P9-CEZ-333

CHRISTMAS COOKING
AROUND THE WORLD

Also by Susan Purdy

CHRISTMAS COOKBOOK
CHRISTMAS GIFTS GOOD ENOUGH TO EAT
HALLOWEEN COOKBOOK
JEWISH HOLIDAY COOKBOOK

A GROLIER COMPANY

CHRISTMAS COOKING AROUND THE WORLD

WRITTEN AND ILLUSTRATED BY
SUSAN PURDY

A Holiday Cookbook

FRANKLIN WATTS
NEW YORK/LONDON/
TORONTO/SYDNEY
1983

16530

Cover photograph by Ginger Giles

Library of Congress Cataloging in Publication Data

Purdy, Susan Gold
Christmas cooking around the world.

(A Holiday cookbook)
Includes index.
Summary: Twenty-six traditional recipes for holiday dishes from the British Isles, France, Italy, Scandinavia, and elsewhere. Includes an introduction to basic cooking skills, descriptions of international Christmas customs, and seven decorative craft projects.

1. Christmas cookery—Juvenile literature. 2. Cookery, International—Juvenile literature. [1. Christmas cookery. 2. Cookery, International. 3. Christmas decorations. 4. Handicraft] I. Title. II. Series.

TX739.P82   1983 641.5′68   83–1334
ISBN 0–531–04654–0
ISBN 0–531–03578–6

For Phoebe

For help in testing and tasting the recipes in this book I want to thank my family, Geoffrey and Cassandra Purdy, as well as Barbara Cover, Diana de Vries, Michele Peasley, and my students (both adults and children) at the Silo Cooking School in New Milford, Connecticut. For recipe research and advice on international celebrations, I am indebted to Robin and Thérèse Davies (England), Sesyle, Andy, and Julia Hine, and Victoria Hine Jones (Italy), Andromaki Valkanos and Efthymios Valkanos (Greece), Anna Olson (Sweden), the late Maria Peterdi (Hungary), and Olga and Wilhelm Dichter (Poland).

The author extends special thanks to Ruth Henderson for permission to photograph the cover of this book using the facilities of the kitchen of The Silo Cooking School, New Milford, Connecticut.

 **CONTENTS**

INTRODUCTION 8

BEFORE YOU BEGIN 10

MEASUREMENTS
Standard and Metric 12

BASIC SKILLS 13
To Level Measurements 13
To Measure Butter or Shortening 13
To Sift Flour 13
To Weigh Flour 14
To Roll Out Dough 14
To Chop an Onion 14
To Knead Yeast Dough 15
To Separate an Egg 16

CHRISTMAS IN THE BRITISH ISLES 17
English Holly Place Cards 20
Egg Nog 21
Individual English Fruitcakes 22
Old English Plum Pudding with Hard Sauce 24
Scotch Hogmanay Shortbread 30

CHRISTMAS IN FRANCE 32
French Epiphany Crown 33
French Christmas Ball (*Coupe de Noël*) 34
French Almond Tile Cookies (*Tuiles Aux Amandes*) 36
Babas au Rhum 38
Three Kings' Cake (*Galette des Rois*) 41

CHRISTMAS IN ITALY 43
Italian Christmas Tree Napkin Holder 44
Italian Christmas Ricotta Cheese Pie (*Torta di Ricotta*) 45

Sienese Nougat Candy (*Panforte di Siena*) 48
Italian Christmas Bread (*Panettone*) 50

CHRISTMAS IN SCANDINAVIA 54
Danish Christmas Hearts 56
Caramelized Potatoes (*Brunede Kartofler*) 57
Danish Sand Cookies (*Sandkager*) 58
Swedish Christmas Rice Porridge (*Risengröd*) 60
Anna Olson's Spritz Cookies (*Spritsar*) 62
Lucia Buns 64

CHRISTMAS IN MIDDLE AND EASTERN EUROPE 67
Czechoslovakian Meringue Decorations 70
Polish Mazurkas (*Mazurek*) 72
Bulgarian Yogurt Cookies (*Masni Kurabii*) 74
Polish Almond Soup (*Zupa Migdałowa*) 75
Greek Nut Cookies (*Kourabiedes*) 76

CHRISTMAS IN GERMANY AND AUSTRIA 78
Austrian Advent Wreath 79
German Spice Cookies (*Pfeffernüsse*) 80
Marzipan-Stuffed Prunes 82
Viennese Nut Crescents (*Butterhörnchen*) 83

CHRISTMAS IN MEXICO 84
Mexican Flowered Napkin Rings 86
Christmas Eve Salad (*Ensalada de Noche Buena*) 87
Empanadas 88
Mexican Nut Cookies (*Pastelitos de Boda*) 91

WRITE YOUR OWN FAMILY COOKBOOK 92

INDEX 95

INTRODUCTION

All over the world, Christmas is the time for sharing love, gifts, and special foods. Families in every country and region have their traditional holiday favorites. What are yours? As you read this book, you will discover specialties from many peoples and places. We hope they will encourage you to think about your own family's specialties. You can write a book of your own after reading the chapter "How To Write Your Own Family's Cookbook"; you will learn how to collect and organize recipes. In the process, you will also learn about your background, your relatives, and yourself. As a bonus, you will create a very special cookbook that everyone in your family will treasure.

As you read this cookbook, you will find introductory chapters describing the customs, foods, and decorations of each area. You will quickly see many similarities among them. This is because many Christmas holiday customs are rooted in pagan (pre-Christian) times and later became part of the Christian religion. As Christianity spread throughout the world, its customs spread with it.

For example, the ancient Romans held a winter festival on the seventeenth day of December, the last month of their year. Called *Saturnalia*, the holiday was in honor of the completion of autumn planting. It was a day of gaiety and freedom, when presents were exchanged. In some provinces, the Romans drew lots to choose a mock "king" to rule during the festival.

In northern Europe, the ancient Teutonic and Celtic tribes also held a winter solstice festival, during their great feast month, December. The celebration lasted twelve days and was called *jól*, or *hjul* (later *yule*) meaning "wheel," the symbol of the changing seasons. Logs were burned and bonfires were lit to frighten away winter's darkness and to encourage the return of the sun. Decorations were made of holly, bay, ivy, mistletoe, and evergreens—all of which bloom throughout winter and so represent continuing strength and life.

Our decorations and the custom of lighting candles and holiday lights are modern traditions that originated with these ancient winter festivals. From the ancient Romans come the customs of exchanging gifts and selecting a party "king" from a drawing of lots, similar to today's custom of choosing the one who gets the hidden token in a portion of cake or bread or pudding.

After reading about the customs of each country, follow the directions given to make a Christmas decoration typical of that region. You can make your own international Christmas fair with foods, flags, and decorations of various nations.

When you follow the recipes, be sure to first read all the way through to the end, so you will know what is involved and how to plan your time. Observe safety precautions. In the introductions to each region, all recipes followed by an asterisk (*) will be found in this book. If you have trouble finding a particular recipe, look in the index. Many of these holiday foods can be made as Christmas gifts from your kitchen. You can make another gift out of the Family Cookbook you compile from your own family's specialties.

BEFORE YOU BEGIN

If the arrangement of these recipes looks different to you, it is. In most recipes, ingredients are listed first, then you are told what to do with them. I have told you what foods to get ready, then listed ingredients (in bold type) and instructions when and where you actually use them. My testers find this method always works; I hope you will agree. I also hope you will have the patience to read all the way through a recipe before starting it. This will help you plan your time as well as your activities.

If you plan to use the metric measurements in this book (they are placed alongside the standard measurements), be sure to read the introductory note on Measurements. If you use the standard measurements, proceed as you ordinarily would.

1. Safety: Keep pot handles turned away from the stove front so pots will not be bumped into and spilled. Turn off oven or stove-top as soon as you are through using it. When pots are removed from stove, place them on a heat-proof surface. To prevent fires, keep potholders, dishtowels, aprons, and your clothes away from stove burners. Keep a fire extinguisher in the kitchen just in case (and learn how to use it).

To prevent accidental cuts, store and wash knives separately from other utensils. Only use blender or food processor with an adult's supervision or permission.

2. Butter: All butter used for the recipes in this book is lightly salted unless otherwise noted, when the recipe will say "unsalted" butter. Margarine can almost always be substituted for butter, and in some recipes both are listed. In recipes that taste much better made with butter, margarine has been left off the ingredients list.

3. Flour: For better nutrition, use *unbleached* all-purpose flour instead of bleached. You will find the word *unbleached* on the front of the flour package. Flour is not sifted unless the recipe specifically calls for it. To sift flour, see Basic Skills.

4. Sugar: Sugar is not sifted unless the recipe specifically calls for it. Turbinado (unrefined) sugar can be substituted for an equal amount of granulated white sugar. To substitute honey for granulated sugar, use about ⅞ as much (1 cup sugar = 250 ml = ⅞ cup honey = 220 ml) *and* use about 3 tablespoons (45 ml) *less* liquid in recipe.

5. Eggs: All eggs used in recipes are large size.

6. About Yeast: Yeast is a living plant; liquid that is too hot will kill it. Dry or compressed yeast should always be added to water that is lukewarm, or comfortable to the touch. *Never* use hot water or the yeast will not work and your bread or cake will not rise.

7. Other health-food substitutions: To increase nutritional value of recipes, you can substitute 1 tablespoon (15 ml) sifted soy flour *plus* 1 tablespoon (15 ml) powdered dry milk *plus* 1 tablespoon (15 ml) wheat germ for an equal amount of flour in all cookie and cake recipes. NOTE: Soy flour causes quicker browning, so if you use it, lower oven temperature about 25°.

8. Flavoring: In the recipes for English Plum Pudding (page 24) and Babas au Rhum (page 38), artificial liquor extracts are called for. In these cases, when made by adults or under adult supervision and approval, alcohol may be substituted; quantities are given in the recipe introductions.

9. The timer: Whenever a recipe gives two times (such as 10 to 12 minutes), set your timer for the first time (10). Test for doneness. If necessary, reset timer for additional time (2 minutes) and cook longer.

10. Oven heat: Oven temperatures vary. It is very rare for the actual temperature inside the oven to be exactly the same as the one you set on the thermostat dial. If your foods do not cook in the time or manner described in the recipe, it may be because your oven is too hot, or not as hot as the heat indicated by your thermostat. To be safe, use a separate oven thermometer (sold in a hardware store) that hangs or sits on the oven shelf. Change the temperature on your outside thermostat dial until the inside oven temperature is correct.

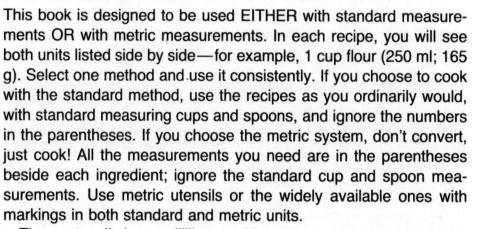

MEASUREMENTS: STANDARD AND METRIC

This book is designed to be used EITHER with standard measurements OR with metric measurements. In each recipe, you will see both units listed side by side—for example, 1 cup flour (250 ml; 165 g). Select one method and use it consistently. If you choose to cook with the standard method, use the recipes as you ordinarily would, with standard measuring cups and spoons, and ignore the numbers in the parentheses. If you choose the metric system, don't convert, just cook! All the measurements you need are in the parentheses beside each ingredient; ignore the standard cup and spoon measurements. Use metric utensils or the widely available ones with markings in both standard and metric units.

These utensils have milliliter markings that are rounded off to the nearest useful whole units. Thus, 1 cup is usually marked 250 ml. You should be aware that this is an approximation. Do not try to figure out apparent irregularities; just use the measurements as they are in this book. All our recipes have been tested with the metric quantities listed, and they work. We have also rounded off our metric quantities to their nearest useful whole units whenever possible.

Practical Examples

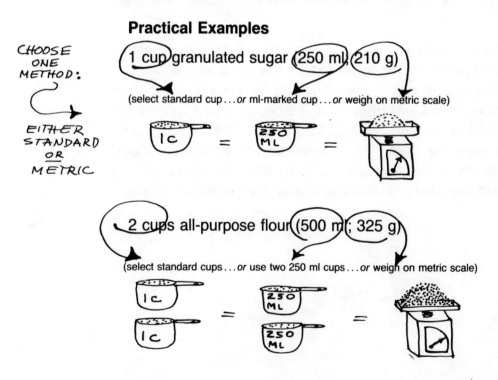

CHOOSE ONE METHOD:

EITHER STANDARD OR METRIC

1 cup granulated sugar (250 ml) (210 g)

(select standard cup . . . or ml-marked cup . . . or weigh on metric scale)

1 C = 250 ML =

2 cups all-purpose flour (500 ml; 325 g)

(select standard cups . . . or use two 250 ml cups . . . or weigh on metric scale)

1 C / 1 C = 250 ML / 250 ML =

BASIC SKILLS

To Level Measurements:

All measurements in this book are level unless otherwise specified. To level a measuring cup or spoon, fill it until slightly mounded, then draw the back of a knife blade over the top, scraping the surface flat.

To Measure Butter or Shortening:

Butter or margarine is easiest to measure when purchased in quarter-pound sticks.

1 pound	= 4 sticks	= 2 cups	= 480 ml	= 480 g
1 stick	= ½ cup	= 8 tablespoons	= 120 ml	= 120 g

Instead of measuring by the stick, you can pack the butter down very firmly into a measuring cup (be sure there are no air spaces trapped in the bottom), or you can use the "water displacement" method: To measure ¼ cup (60 ml) butter, fill a 1-cup (250 ml) measuring cup ¾ full (185 ml) with cold water. Add pieces of butter until the water reaches the 1-cup (250 ml) mark. Pour off water and you are left with ¼ cup (60 ml) measured butter.

To Sift Flour:

Sifting lightens the texture of baked goods. You can use either a strainer or a sifter for this process. Flour is sifted only where the recipe specifically calls for it.

Sift the required amount of flour onto a sheet of wax paper. Then pick up the paper, pull the edges around into a sort of funnel, and *gently* pour as much flour as you need back into a measuring cup. You can also use a spoon to transfer flour. Do not shake or pack measured flour. Level top of cup with knife blade, then add flour to recipe. Or return re-measured flour to sifter, add other dry ingredients, such as baking powder and salt, and sift everything together into the other ingredients in recipe.

To Weigh Flour:

Sift flour onto a piece of wax paper as explained above. Then spoon sifted flour lightly onto your wax-paper-lined scale until the measure is correct.

To Roll Out Dough:

There are two ways to roll out dough. One is on a countertop or a pastry board, the other between sheets of wax paper. If you are using a countertop or a pastry board, spread it lightly with flour so the dough will not stick. Also flour the rolling pin. Then roll out the dough, adding more flour if dough sticks. Some pastry boards and rolling pins are covered with cotton cloth (called a sock) to help prevent sticking; cloths should also be floured.

The second method is to cut two pieces of wax paper, each roughly 14″ (36 cm) long. Place one piece flat on the counter and flour it lightly. Place dough on floured paper, then sprinkle a little flour on top of dough. Cover dough with second paper. Use rolling pin (un-floured) to roll out dough between the papers. Peel the paper off and put it back on again if it gets too wrinkled. When dough is correct thickness, peel top paper off dough.

To Chop an Onion:

"Chopping" with this method means you actually cut the onion into dice, or small pieces. First peel the onion. Then cut the onion in half lengthwise, from root to stem (a). Place one half, cut side down, on board. Hold it with fingers gripping sides, root end to the left (if you are right-handed). Slice onion as shown (b), with point of knife facing root end. Cut almost, but not all the way, through root end; this will help hold onion together. Finally, make narrow cuts in the opposite direction (c), cutting across the first slices to produce the "chopped" or diced pieces. Keep moving your fingers back away from the knife.

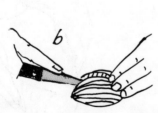
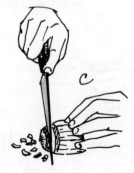

To Knead Yeast Dough:

Sprinkle about ¼ cup flour over pastry board, marble slab, or counter. Sprinkle flour on your clean hands. Turn dough out onto floured area. Fold dough in half toward you, then push it away while leaning on it with the heels of your hands. Give dough a quarter-turn and repeat the folding and pushing. The flour from the board will soon work itself into the dough. Add more flour, a little at a time, until dough no longer feels sticky. Continue folding and pushing dough 5 to 10 minutes, until it looks and feels quite smooth and is no longer sticky to the touch. You may see bubbles stretched across, or under, the skin of the dough. NOTE: You may find it easier to knead half or one third of the dough at a time.

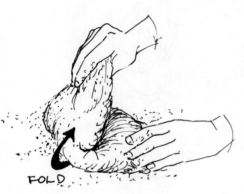

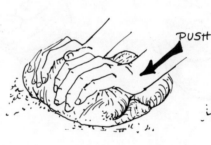

To Separate an Egg:

Here are two different ways to separate an egg. The first method may be new to you, but try it anyway. It is very easy, never breaks the yolk, and is a lot of fun.

First wash your hands, as you will be touching the egg. Crack egg in half by tapping it sharply against side of bowl. Hold egg on its side as shown, grasping ends with your fingers. Fit tips of thumbs into crack. Pull shells apart and *at the same time* turn one half shell upright so it contains all the egg. Hold this shell, containing egg, upright with one hand while the other hand discards the empty half shell. Then turn empty hand palm up, fingers together, over a clean dry bowl. Pour out the entire egg onto the fingers of the empty hand. Spread fingers apart very slightly to let the egg white drip between them into the bowl while the yolk rests on top of the fingers as shown. Collect all of the white in a bowl; put yolk in a separate bowl.

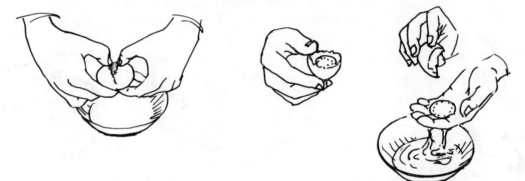

The most common procedure is to break egg in half, then hold half shell containing the yolk upright in one hand while you pour the egg white from the other half shell into a bowl. Then tip yolk out into the empty shell while white that surrounded it falls into bowl below. Place yolk in separate bowl.

CHRISTMAS IN THE BRITISH ISLES

For the purposes of this brief culinary tour, the British Isles consists of England, Scotland, Wales, and Ireland. Many symbols of Christmas in this region were handed down to us by the ancient Druids, who lived in this part of the world long before Christ's birth. Druids worshiped nature and they especially honored holly as a sign of immortality because it remained green and bore red berries in the winter. The parasitic plant called mistletoe symbolized great strength because it lived off the trees it grew upon. Druids also believed mistletoe had the power to protect people from evil, and they hung bunches of it to decorate their dwellings during the midwinter holiday.

Just as the early Norse tribes burned "yule" logs to frighten away the forces of winter darkness in the region now called Scandinavia, so the Druids in the British Isles burned oak or fruitwood logs at their midwinter festival, in the hope that the logs would flame forever, like the sun. This is the origin of the British custom of burning a yule log. During the Middle Ages, a huge green log was burned in the fireplace of the great dining hall on Christmas Eve and the banquet had to last as long as the log burned!

Modern Christmas festivities contain many of these ancient customs. One of these is the drinking of wassail, a hot spiced wine punch flavored with tiny roasted apples or clove-stuck oranges. This drink comes from the early Saxon tribes of Britain who drank it while toasting "*wæs hæl*," "to your health." Midday on Christmas Eve is the time to begin the traditional Wassail Party, at which this hot punch or wassail is served.

In the evening, the British generally have a family Christmas Eve dinner, then place gifts beneath a decorated tree before going to a special midnight church service. Before children go to sleep that night, they hang a stocking at the foot of their bed or by the fireplace. During the night, Father Christmas arrives and, leaving his reindeer and sleigh on the roof, comes down the chimney with a sack full of toys. While he fills the stockings, he enjoys a glass of sherry and perhaps a mince pie left for him by thoughtful parents.

On Christmas morning, children wake up early to see if their stockings are full. They cannot wait to open these presents! After a light breakfast, many families go to a morning church service, then return to open the gifts under their tree. By one o'clock the entire family— uncles, aunts, cousins, grandparents—have gathered for the holiday banquet: a heavily laden "groaning board" of traditional foods. The main course will usually be a roast turkey stuffed with chestnuts at one end and herb stuffing at the other. The turkey is usually served with giblet gravy, bread sauce, small sausages, bacon, roasted *and* mashed potatoes, and brussel sprouts.

The dessert is usually the famous Christmas Pudding, also called Plum Pudding*. This hot, rich dessert, trimmed with fresh holly leaves, arrives at the table smoldering in blue flames of burning brandy—a dramatic presentation that can startle you into waking up and eating more just when you thought you were filled to bursting. The pudding, served with a creamy butter-sugar-brandy sauce, may, if old traditions are followed, contain a hidden coin that will bring good luck to the finder. You were tricked if you thought the plum pudding was the last course! It is fast followed by a selection of mince pies (spicy mixtures of chopped suet and fruits), bowls of dried fruits, Stilton cheese, and nuts.

The banquet often ends with games, prizes, and "crackers," which are crepe-paper-covered tubes that make a "crack" noise when the end-tabs are pulled out. Inside the crackers are favors and jokes or riddles.

In the afternoon, the family gathers by the radio or television to hear the monarch's short annual Christmas message to the nation. It is not long before teatime offers yet another customary treat: a rich, dark Fruitcake* called Christmas Cake. In the north of England it is served plain or trimmed with marzipan, candied fruits, and dried nuts; in the south it is frosted twice: first with a layer of marzipan, and then with a rough coat of royal icing that resembles snow. Finally it is topped with little figurines such as a Christmas tree or Father Christmas (Santa Claus) with his reindeer. Later that same evening, the light supper features sausage rolls (small spicy sausages wrapped in pastry) and more mince pies.

* Whenever an asterisk appears, it indicates that the recipe marked appears in this book.

The day after Christmas is called Boxing Day, the time when friends and neighbors visit. Originally, this was the day when tradespeople who worked for the family came around to collect their annual gift in a Christmas box; hence, the name of the holiday. Boxing Day diners eat Christmas Day leftovers, the most notable of which has the delightful name of "Bubble and Squeak." It is made from mashed potatoes and brussel sprouts mixed together and then fried in shortening until the mixture forms a browned, crisp cake.

New Year's Day brings its own customs and foods. In some parts of the British Isles, a favorite New Year's drink is Egg Nog,* a frothy egg-milk drink topped with nutmeg. In Scotland, New Year's Eve is called *Hogmanay*. On this night, one serves a New Year's Black Bun, a dark fruitcake made into a ball wrapped in a pastry crust.

The Scots also have a tradition called "First Footing," whereby the family's luck in the New Year is determined by whomever is the first guest to set foot (first foot) in the door after the New Year strikes. It is extremely bad luck for the first footer to be a woman, a light-haired man, or an undertaker. A chimney sweep brings the most luck of all. However, any dark-haired man will bring good luck and is the one chosen to go outside, then cross the threshold back into the house at the stroke of midnight. For added good luck, the first footer must carry a gift of food as he comes in. This may be a special cake called Hogmanay Shortbread,* or bread, salt, or an orange. But the most important things he must always carry are a bottle of Scotch whiskey and a piece of coal—to ensure both good cheer and heat throughout the winter.

ENGLISH HOLLY PLACE CARDS

Holly was worshiped by the ancient Druids as a symbol of immortality because it remained green throughout the winter. In some parts of England, it is said that bees hum a carol on Christmas Day in honor of the Christ Child. Holly is placed on the hives to wish the bees a Merry Christmas.

Make these festive holly-shaped place cards for your holiday table.

Materials: Red and green construction paper, ruler, pencil, scissors, rubber cement, felt-tip pen.

1. For each place card you need three leaves, one base strip, and three red berries. To make one leaf, cut out green paper in the shape shown, roughly 3½" long by 1" wide (9 × 2.5 cm). Use the first leaf as a pattern for the others. Cut as many as needed. Cut each base strip 6" long by ¾" wide (15 × 2 cm) from green paper. To make the red berries, fold red paper in thirds and cut circles roughly ⅜" (1 cm) in diameter.

2. To make the base, fold over a small flap on one short end of the green paper strip (a). Keeping this piece bent over, fold the remaining strip into thirds, as shown (b). Press on folds. Stand up triangle and glue flap to base (arrow, c).

3. Write a guest's name on a leaf vertically, as shown. To complete one place card, glue the name-leaf to one leg of the base strip. Glue the bottom edges of two other leaves to each side, as shown. Glue three red berries over the glued leaf ends. Stand holly place card on table.

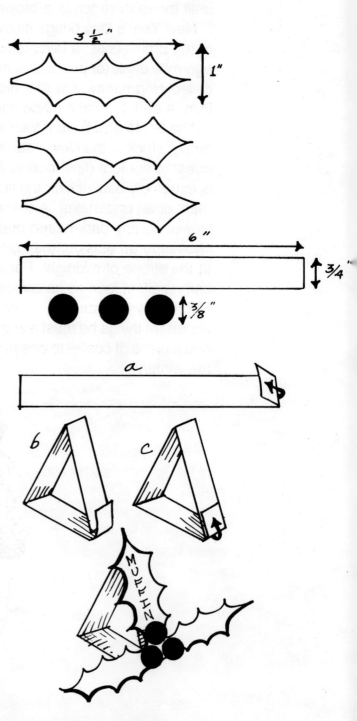

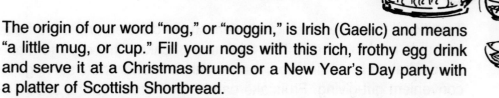

EGG NOG

The origin of our word "nog," or "noggin," is Irish (Gaelic) and means "a little mug, or cup." Fill your nogs with this rich, frothy egg drink and serve it at a Christmas brunch or a New Year's Day party with a platter of Scottish Shortbread.

NOTE: This recipe can be doubled or tripled; the more eggs you use, the richer the mixture.

EQUIPMENT:
Measuring cups and spoons
Punch bowl
Medium and large mixing bowls
Electric mixer or egg beater
Rubber scraper
Ladle
Punch cups or mugs
Nutmeg grater

FOODS YOU WILL NEED:
3 or 4 eggs
4 to 6 tablespoons confectioners' sugar (60–90 ml), or honey or maple syrup
1½ teaspoons vanilla extract (7.5 ml)
1 quart homogenized milk (1 L)
Several pinches nutmeg, freshly grated

Ingredients:

(To make four 1-cup servings [250 ml])

3 or 4 eggs (the more eggs, the richer the drink)

4 to 6 tablespoons confectioners' sugar (60–90 ml)
1½ teaspoons vanilla extract (7.5 ml)
1 quart homogenized milk (1 L)
Nutmeg

How To:

1. Separate eggs (see Basic Skills). Place whites in medium-sized mixing bowl and yolks in large mixing bowl. Use electric mixer or egg beater to beat whites until they stand by themselves in stiff peaks.

2. Measure sugar into yolks—amount of sugar depends on your taste. Add vanilla and beat well. Beat in milk. Taste and add more sugar if necessary. Pour mixture into punch bowl and use rubber scraper to "spoon" egg whites into mixture. Stir or fold them in slightly. Egg whites should form small mounds floating in the egg nog.

3. To serve, ladle egg nog plus egg whites into mugs and top with freshly grated nutmeg.

INDIVIDUAL ENGLISH FRUITCAKES

Traditional fruitcakes are rich confections of candied and dried fruits and nuts held together with a minimum of cake. This easy-to-make recipe, baked in muffin cups, makes cakes for individual servings or convenient gift-giving. Fruitcake can be prepared months ahead of the holidays and frozen (wrapped in foil) or stored in airtight tins in a cool, dry place.

EQUIPMENT:
Measuring cups and spoons
Electric mixer
Large mixing bowl
Sifter
Muffin tins (2½″ diameter [6 cm])
Paper or foil muffin tin liners
Cake tester or toothpick
Wire rack

FOODS YOU WILL NEED:
1 cup butter or margarine, at room temperature (2 sticks; 240 g)
1 pound box light brown sugar (2⅓ cups; 450 g)
4 eggs
2⅓ cups plus ⅓ cup all-purpose flour (580 plus 80 ml; 380 plus 55 g)
1 teaspoon baking powder (5 ml)
1 cup apple cider, white grape juice, or other fruit juice (250 ml)
1 cup seedless raisins (160 g)
1 cup dried currants (100 g)
1 cup diced citron or chopped mixed candied fruits (200 g)
1 cup candied cherries, cut up or whole (227 g)
1 cup dried and pitted dates, chopped (200 g)
1 cup dried figs or apricots, cut up, or use half and half (180 g)
1½ cups walnuts, chopped (185 g)

Ingredients:

(To make 36 to 40 cakes, 2½″ diameter [6 cm])

1 cup butter or margarine, at room temperature (2 sticks; 240 g)

1 pound box light brown sugar (2⅓ cups; 450 g)

How To:

1. Preheat oven to 300°F (150° C). Set liners in muffin cups. (Or, grease and flour muffin cups.) In large bowl of electric mixer, beat butter or margarine until creamy. Add sugar and beat until light and smooth.

4 eggs
2⅓ cups all-purpose flour, sifted (580 ml; 380 g)
1 teaspoon baking powder (5 ml)
1 cup apple cider, white grape juice, or other fruit juice (250 ml)

⅓ cup all-purpose flour (80 ml; 55 g)
1 cup seedless raisins (160 g)
1 cup dried currants (100 g)
1 cup diced citron or chopped mixed candied fruits (200 g)
1 cup candied cherries, cut or whole (227 g)
1 cup dried and pitted dates, chopped (200 g)
1 cup dried figs or apricots, cut up, or use half and half (180 g)
1½ cups walnuts, chopped (185 g)

LINERS

2. One at a time, add eggs to a measuring cup, then add to butter-sugar mixture and beat well. Sift 2⅓ cups flour and baking powder onto mixture. Add a little cider or juice and beat slowly. Add remaining liquid and beat until batter is well mixed.

3. In large mixing bowl, sprinkle ⅓ cup flour over dried fruits and nuts. Mix with your hands to distribute flour and separate sticky fruit pieces. Then stir this mixture into the batter.

4. Spoon batter into prepared muffin cups, filling nearly to the top. Make a mound in the center, as the mixture does not rise very much. Bake at 300°F (150°C) for 40 to 45 minutes, or until golden brown and a cake tester placed in center of a cake comes out clean. Remove cakes from tin and cool on wire rack. To store, wrap airtight in foil or plastic bag and freeze, or keep in a cool place.
NOTE: You can also bake this cake in tube or loaf pans (buttered and floured) instead of muffin cups. Baking time will be slightly longer, depending on pan size.

OLD ENGLISH PLUM PUDDING
WITH HARD SAUCE

In England, this famous dessert is often simply called Christmas Pudding. It is the traditional grand finale for the Christmas banquet. Brought to the table as the dining room lights are dimmed, it glows with blue flames from the burning brandy, and is decorated with a sprig of holly. It is served with a dollop of butter-sugar Hard Sauce. A long-ago custom still observed in some parts of England is the hiding of silver charms or sixpence coins (wrapped in foil) in the batter before steaming the pudding. Whoever finds the charm or coin gets good luck.

Whether or not you add charms, you must observe this Old English tradition: When making the batter, every member of the family takes a turn stirring—*always in a clockwise direction* (to avoid bad luck) while he or she makes a secret wish. Plum Pudding takes time to prepare as the fruits require an hour of soaking. Plan your time accordingly.

To give the flavors of the many ingredients time to mature, plum pudding is often made as early as the first of November and stored, wrapped airtight, in a cool place until the holidays. At intervals during the waiting period, the cake is unwrapped, poked with a knitting needle, and sprinkled with brandy to give it flavor (not recommended for children). In our experience, it is also delicious without brandy, and when made just before serving. Puddings may also be frozen. In any case, they are always resteamed to heat them through just before serving on Christmas Day.

NOTE: Adults may prefer to substitute ¼ to ⅓ cup (60–80 ml) brandy or sweet sherry for extract in the Hard Sauce. See note 8, page 11.

EQUIPMENT:
Measuring cups and spoons
Food processor or meat grinder
Large, medium, and small mixing bowls
Grater
Wax paper
Nut chopper
Mixing spoons
Molds: 4 one-pint (½ L) heat-proof molds, or
  2 one-quart (1 L) molds or heat-proof bowls,
  or bread pans of equivalent size
Steamer: large Dutch oven with lid and rack or
  ring-shaped steamer rack with feet (*bain
  marie*), or small heat-proof pan set in
  bottom of pot to lift mold
Aluminum foil
Cotton string
Scissors
Cake tester
Potholders
Knife with narrow blade
Soup ladle or small syrup server
Serving platter
Serving bowl and spoon for Hard Sauce
Fresh holly sprig (optional)
Matches for flaming brandy to serve pudding

FOODS YOU WILL NEED:
1 cup suet, finely ground (buy it in hunks from
  butcher who will grind it for you, or do it
  yourself in food processor or meat grinder)
  (¼ lb; 130 g)
½ cup dates, chopped (100 g)
¾ cup seedless raisins (120 g)
½ cup golden raisins (65 g)
¼ cup currants (25 g)
¼ cup candied citron, chopped (50 g)
¼ cup candied mixed fruit, chopped (50 g)
1 medium-large apple, peeled, cored, and
  chopped (1 cup; 120 g)
1 lemon—grated rind plus juice
1½ cups cranberry juice, cider, or other fruit
  juice, or buttermilk (375 ml)
4 eggs
1¼ cups dark brown sugar, packed (310 ml;
  315 g)
2 tablespoons molasses, unsulphured (30 ml)
½ cup walnuts, chopped (65 g)
½ cup fine dry breadcrumbs, unseasoned
  (70 g)
1 cup all-purpose flour (250 ml; 165 g) plus a
  little extra for sprinkling on suet
1 teaspoon salt (5 ml)
1½ teaspoons baking powder (7.5 ml)
¾ teaspoon baking soda (4 ml)
¼ teaspoon mace (1.2 ml)
1 teaspoon cinnamon (5 ml)
¼ teaspoon ground cloves (1.2 ml)
½ teaspoon ground allspice (2.5 ml)
½ teaspoon nutmeg (2.5 ml)

Hard Sauce:
1 cup butter at room temperature (2 sticks; 240
  g)
1 pound box confectioners' sugar (4½ cups;
  455 g)
1 to 2 teaspoons brandy extract or rum extract
  (5–10 ml or to taste) plus enough milk or
  cream (about 3 tablespoons, 45 ml) to
  soften mixture

Ingredients:	How To:

(To make four pint-sized [½ L] or two one-quart [1 L] pudding molds)
1 cup suet, packed (¼ lb; 130 g)

1. Ask butcher to chop suet for you or cut it into small lumps, sprinkle it with a little flour, and grind it in the food processor or meat grinder. Remove any membranes you see. Pack cup firmly when measuring suet. Set suet aside.

½ cup dates, chopped (100 g)
¾ cup seedless raisins (120 g)
½ cup golden raisins (65 g)
¼ cup currants (25 g)
¼ cup candied citron, chopped (50 g)
¼ cup candied mixed fruit, chopped (50 g)
1 medium-large apple, peeled, cored, chopped (1 cup; 120 g)
1 lemon
1½ cups cranberry juice, cider, or other juice, or buttermilk (375 ml)

2. In *medium* mixing bowl, combine all dried and candied fruits and peel. Peel, core, chop, and add apple. Grate lemon peel onto wax paper; add peel to bowl. Squeeze lemon juice into a measuring cup, remove pits, add juice to bowl. Add fruit juice, stir, and let stand about 1 hour, to soften fruit, while you prepare other ingredients and molds.

4 eggs
1¼ cups dark brown sugar, packed (310 ml; 315 g)
2 tablespoons molasses, unsulphured (30 ml)

3. In *small* bowl, beat eggs, brown sugar, and molasses, and set aside.

½ cup walnuts, chopped (65 g)

½ cup fine dry breadcrumbs, unseasoned (70 g)

1 cup all-purpose flour (250 ml; 165 g)

1 teaspoon salt (5 ml)

1½ teaspoons baking powder (7.5 ml)

¾ teaspoon baking soda (4 ml)

¼ teaspoon mace (1.2 ml)

1 teaspoon cinnamon (5 ml)

¼ teaspoon ground cloves (1.2 ml)

½ teaspoon ground allspice (2.5 ml)

½ teaspoon nutmeg (2.5 ml)

4. Chop nuts. Put them in *largest* mixing bowl. Add ground suet and stir in breadcrumbs. Sift in flour, salt, baking powder, and soda. Add spices. Stir in egg-brown sugar mixture. Stir in the soaked mixture of fruits and liquid.

Now *stir* in CLOCKWISE direction for good luck, and make a wish as you do so. Invite all members of your family to have a turn and make a wish. This insures a successful pudding!

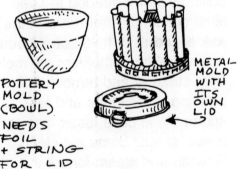

POTTERY MOLD (BOWL) NEEDS FOIL + STRING FOR LID

METAL-MOLD WITH ITS OWN LID

5. To prepare 4 one-pint or 2 one-quart molds, grease them generously with butter or margarine. Also grease sheets of foil for mold covers, and set out lengths of cotton string to tie foil onto molds. Prepare your steamer. Find a small pan or heat-proof object that can sit on pot bottom to hold your mold during steaming. Be sure steaming pot has tight-fitting lid. Fill steamer about ½ full with boiling water, cover and set on low heat until ready to use.

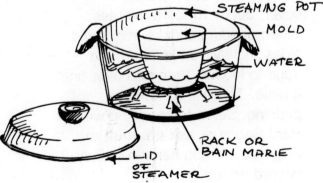

STEAMING POT

MOLD

WATER

RACK OR BAIN MARIE

LID OF STEAMER

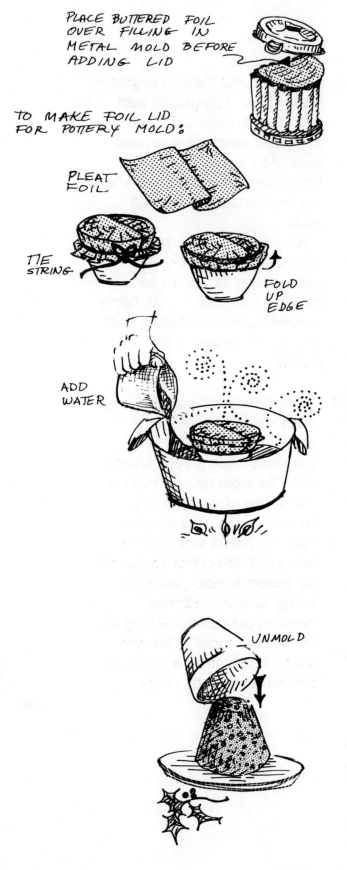

PLACE BUTTERED FOIL OVER FILLING IN METAL MOLD BEFORE ADDING LID

TO MAKE FOIL LID FOR POTTERY MOLD:

PLEAT FOIL

TIE STRING

FOLD UP EDGE

ADD WATER

UNMOLD

6. Spoon batter into greased molds, filling ¾ full. Batter rises about 1″ (2.5 cm) during baking, so leave room.

Fold a pleat in well-buttered foil as shown (to allow room for rising), then press foil (buttered side down) over mold top and tie with string. Fold foil edge up over string.

Ask an adult to help set full mold into steamer, carefully balancing it on rack. Add boiling water until it reaches about half or two thirds of the way up the side of your mold. Cover steamer, bring to a boil, then lower heat and boil very slowly for about three hours. Add more boiling water if needed to keep level constant. After three hours **ask an adult** to help see if pudding is done. With potholders, lift mold from steamer and remove foil: pudding should look and feel spongy, and cake tester inserted in center should come out clean. Rewrap and steam longer if needed. When done, remove from steamer and cool, without foil cover, about 10 to 15 minutes. When pudding shrinks from mold sides slightly, run knife around edge to loosen, then turn over onto a plate. This will unmold the pudding. Serve hot pudding with Hard Sauce or **ask an adult** to help serve it with flaming brandy poured on top.

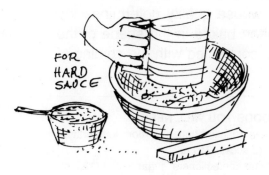

FOR HARD SAUCE

Hard Sauce:
(To make about 2 cups [500 ml])
1 cup butter (2 sticks; 240 g), at room temperature
1 pound box confectioners' sugar, sifted (4½ cups; 455 g)
1 to 2 teaspoons brandy extract or rum extract (5–10 ml or to taste) plus enough milk or cream (about 3 tablespoons, 45 ml) to soften mixture until creamy

7. NOTE: If pudding is frozen, defrost it for several hours before dinnertime. Two hours before serving, pudding must be resteamed, to heat through. If pudding was not stored in its original mold, butter a clean mold (or similar container that will protect pudding from water during steaming) and place pudding inside. Seal top with buttered foil and steam for two hours as in step 6. Unmold onto serving plate.

8. To make Hard Sauce, beat butter until soft with electric mixer. Sift in confectioners' sugar and beat very slowly until combined. Add flavoring. Store in refrigerator, tightly covered, until ready to serve.

To Flame Pudding:
Measure about ¼ cup brandy into small pan or syrup server and set over heat on stove until warmed through. Be sure pudding is hot, on serving plate, and ready to be served. When brandy is hot, **ask an adult** to touch a match to brandy and pour it immediately over hot pudding in front of guests. Serve as soon as flames have burned down. Most of the alcohol burns off so it will not harm or intoxicate you.

SCOTCH HOGMANAY SHORTBREAD

Hogmanay is the Scottish name for New Year's Eve, and shortbread is one of the foods traditionally carried over the threshold by the "first-footer," the first person entering one's home after the New Year strikes. A rich and irresistible thick butter cookie, shortbread is made only with the finest unsalted butter, whose quality determines the flavor of the finished product. It is often baked in the shape of the sun, a survival of pagan sun worship connected with the coming of the new year.

EQUIPMENT:
Measuring cups and spoons
Mixing bowl and large spoon, or electric mixer
Sifter
Cookie sheet
Ruler
Paring knife
Table fork
Flat serving plate
Spatula

FOODS YOU WILL NEED:
1 cup unsalted butter, at room temperature
  (2 sticks; 240 g)
½ cup confectioners' sugar, sifted (125 ml;
  65 g)
2 cups all-purpose flour, sifted (500 ml; 270 g)
½ teaspoon salt (2.5 ml)

Ingredients:

(To make one cake 8″ in diameter [20 cm] containing 8 servings)

1 cup unsalted butter, at room temperature (2 sticks; 240 g)
½ cup confectioners' sugar (125 ml; 65 g)
2 cups all-purpose flour, sifted (500 ml; 270 g)
½ teaspoon salt (2.5 ml)

How To:

1. Preheat oven to 325°F (165°C). In bowl, sift sugar over butter and mix together well using large spoon or electric mixer. Sift on flour and salt and slowly mix until just blended. Do *not* overwork dough or cookie will not be tender and flaky.

2. Flour your hands, then lift dough ball from bowl and set on ungreased cookie sheet. With your hands, press dough into a flat round cake, about ¾″ (2 cm) thick and 8″ (20 cm) in diameter.

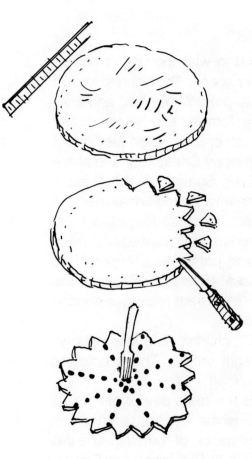

3. Notch edges of cake with knife, as shown, to make sun's rays. Divide the sun into eight equal wedges by pricking with fork tines as shown. These lines make the cake easy to cut after baking.

4. Bake shortbread at 325°F (165°C) for about 40 to 45 minutes, or until evenly golden. When cool, use spatula to slide cake onto a flat plate. Store airtight. Serve cut into wedges. Warm in oven to recrisp if needed.

WEDGE

CHRISTMAS IN FRANCE

In French homes, Christmas is ushered in with the young people setting up a miniature *crèche*, or manger scene. The figures, known as *santons*, represent all the animals, angels, Wise Men, and Holy Family of the nativity. On Christmas Eve, families and friends gather to go to midnight mass and visit the church *crèche*. Then they return home, wish each other a *Joyeux Noël* (Happy Christmas) and share the feast of *Le Réveillon* (Christmas Eve). Sometimes this feast is eaten before midnight mass, but either way, a traditional menu in the city of Paris might consist of oysters, white sausages, a meat pie called *Tourtière*, roast partridge or turkey with roasted or puréed chestnuts, and several desserts including petits fours, Almond Tile Cookies* (*Tuiles aux Amandes*), Rum Cake* (*Babas au Rhum*), fruits, a yule log cake (*Bûche de Noël*), and an ice cream-meringue sundae called a Christmas Ball* (*Coupe de Noël*).

On Christmas Day (*Le Jour de Noël*), children find little gifts left in the shoes they have set out the night before. These gifts are brought by Father Christmas (*Le Père Noël*).

New Year's Day (*Le Jour de l'An*) is the main day of gift-giving, when presents are exchanged by the whole family. January 6 is Epiphany, which commemorates the Adoration of the Magi, the day the Three Kings are said to have arrived in Bethlehem. In France, there is a festive Epiphany dinner that concludes with the Three Kings' Cake* (*Galette des Rois*). Inside the cake is a hidden surprise: a tiny china doll (*Jésus*) or a dry bean (which is safer for your teeth). Whoever finds the doll or bean in his or her portion of cake is chosen the king or queen, given a gold paper crown, and presides over the rest of the party.

FRENCH EPIPHANY CROWN

This gold paper crown can form the centerpiece for your Epiphany party table. Later, it can be worn by the queen or king who finds the bean in the Three Kings' Cake (*Galette des Rois*).

Materials: Gold craft foil (or stiff gold paper), pencil, ruler, scissors, glue or stapler, bits of colored paper or sequins for trimming.

1. Cut strip of gold paper 3″ by 24″ (7.5 × 60 cm). On one long edge draw and then cut out pointed designs such as the ones shown.

2. Glue bits of colored paper or sequins on strip for trimming.

3. Pull short ends around. Overlap them about 2″ or 3″ (5 or 7.5 cm), and staple or glue ends to hold crown together. Set crown in center of party table. In the middle of the crown, you can place a small vase filled with evergreen or holly branches. When the king or queen of the party is chosen, "crown" that person with the gold centerpiece, leaving the greens to decorate the table.

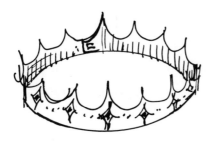

FRENCH CHRISTMAS BALL
(COUPE DE NOËL)

This special dessert is an ice cream sundae set upon a crisp meringue nest and topped with candied chestnuts. Chestnuts appear in many forms during the Christmas holidays in France—roasted with turkey, boiled as a vegetable, and candied in syrup as used in this recipe. *Marrons Glacés*, as they are called, can be bought bottled in gourmet or specialty food shops. Meringue nests are easy to prepare but take at least an hour to bake, so allow enough time (or make them ahead and store or freeze them until needed).

NOTE: This recipe uses four egg whites. The yolks can be used to make Three Kings' Cake, page 41.

EQUIPMENT:
Cookie sheets
Brown paper bag
Scissors
Measuring cups and spoons
Electric mixer
Rubber scraper
Soup spoon
Pancake turner
Wire rack
Ice cream scoop (optional)

FOODS YOU WILL NEED:
Butter and flour—to prepare papered cookie
    sheets
4 egg whites
Dash of salt
Pinch of cream of tartar
½ teaspoon vanilla extract (2.5 ml)
⅔ cup confectioners' sugar, sifted (160 ml;
    90 g)
Vanilla ice cream—one scoop per serving
Candied chestnuts in syrup (*Marrons Glacés*,
    bought in gourmet or specialty shops)
Maraschino cherries and holly leaves (optional,
    for garnish)

Ingredients:

(To make 12 servings or 12 meringue "nests" each 3" [7.5 cm] in diameter)

4 egg whites
Dash of salt
Pinch of cream of tartar

How To:

1. Cut a brown paper bag so it opens flat. Then cut paper to line your cookie sheets. Press paper flat. Butter paper, then dust it with flour and shake off excess. Set lined cookie sheets aside.

2. Preheat oven to 225°F (110°C). Be sure bowl and beaters of mixer are absolutely clean and free of grease. Add egg whites, dash of salt, and pinch of cream of tartar to mixer bowl. Beat on high speed until whites get very foamy—but not yet stiff.

½ teaspoon vanilla extract (2.5 ml)

⅔ cup confectioners' sugar, sifted (160 ml; 90 g)

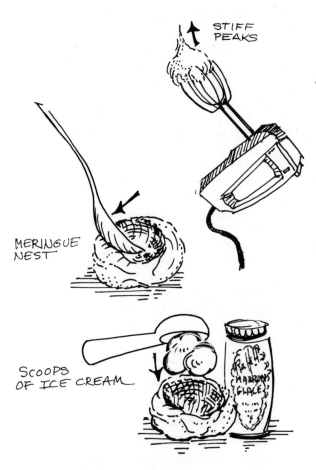

STIFF PEAKS

MERINGUE NEST

SCOOPS OF ICE CREAM

Vanilla ice cream
Candied chestnuts in syrup (Marrons Glacés)
Maraschino cherries (optional)
Holly leaves (optional)

3. Turn off mixer. Add vanilla and sift into bowl about half the sugar. Beat again. Stop mixer and add rest of sugar and beat until whites are very stiff. Stop mixer and hold up beater upside down—whites should form a peak that does *not* droop.

4. Use soup spoon to drop lumps of meringue onto the prepared baking sheet. You should make about twelve "nests," each about the width of a teacup. Use back of spoon to hollow out center of each nest and push up side edges.

5. Bake meringues in preheated 225°F (110°C) oven for 45 to 60 minutes. Meringue should bake slowly until dried out and crisp. If not thoroughly dry, bake an extra 20 to 30 minutes. When done, meringue should look white or *slightly* beige-tan in color. Use spatula to lift off warm nests. Set them to cool on wire rack. If they stick to paper, moisten spatula with hot water *or* dampen *underside* of brown paper with moist sponge and wait a minute for moisture to penetrate before you lift off nests.

6. To serve, put each meringue nest on a serving dish, cover with a scoop of vanilla ice cream, and top with a tablespoon of candied chestnuts in syrup. For a holiday touch, you can also add a red maraschino cherry and a sprig of holly.

FRENCH ALMOND TILE COOKIES
(TUILES AUX AMANDES)

These deliciously crisp cookies have a curved shape that resembles the French roofing tiles for which they are named. They are very easy and quick to prepare, but an adult's help may be necessary to shape the cookies as they are handled while still warm from baking. Traditionally they are set over a broom handle to mold into shape! The recipe makes about two dozen cookies but it can be doubled.

NOTE: The cookies taste just as good flat if you prefer not to mold them into a curved shape.

EQUIPMENT:
Measuring cups and spoons
Small frying pan
Nut chopper, food processor, or blender
Large mixing bowl and mixing spoon
Cookie sheets
2 teaspoons
Wooden spoon
Table fork
Glass of water
Pancake turner
Cookie shaper: broom handle covered with foil or a clean tea towel, set across a table, or curved French bread pan, or rolling pin

FOODS YOU WILL NEED:
⅔ cup almonds, blanched, toasted, and chopped (100 g)
1 cup plus 1 tablespoon confectioners' sugar, sifted (265 ml; 110 g)
¼ cup all-purpose flour, sifted (60 ml; 40 g)
1 egg plus 1 egg white
2 tablespoons unsalted butter, *very* soft but not quite melted (30 ml); plus extra for greasing pans
Pinch of salt
½ teaspoon vanilla extract (2.5 ml)

Ingredients:

*(To make about 28 cookies 3"
[7.5 cm] in diameter)*
⅔ cup almonds, blanched (100 g)
1 cup plus 1 tablespoon confectioners' sugar, sifted (265 ml; 110 g)
¼ cup all-purpose flour, sifted (60 ml; 40 g)
1 egg plus 1 egg white
2 tablespoons unsalted butter, *very* soft but not quite melted (30 ml)
Pinch of salt
½ teaspoon vanilla extract (2.5 ml)

How To:

1. Preheat oven to 400°F (204°C). Butter cookie sheets and set them aside. Measure almonds into frying pan and set on medium heat. Stir with wooden spoon, watching constantly, for a few minutes—*just* until almonds *begin* to turn color and look golden. Remove from heat, cool, and chop them in nut chopper, food processor, or blender. Place nuts in mixing bowl.

2. Sift sugar and flour over nuts in bowl. Stir to combine. Add egg

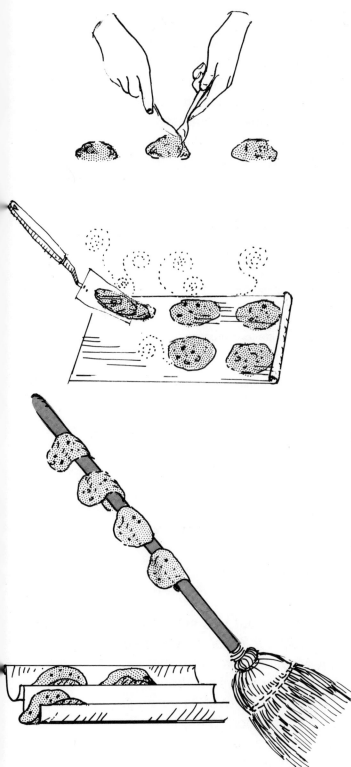

plus egg white, butter (be sure it is not stiff and cold), salt, and vanilla. Mix well until batter is blended.

3. Drop batter by heaping teaspoonsful on buttered cookie sheets. Since the cookies "grow" during baking, leave at least the space of four fingers between cookies. Dip fork in water and press tines on centers of any "fat" cookies. They must be evenly flat to bake properly.

4. Set cookies in 400°F (204°C) oven and bake 4 to 6 minutes, or *just* until edges look golden brown. It is best to peek into oven to check!

5. While *tuiles* are baking, set out broom handle (well balanced on table and covered with foil or a clean tea towel), or use a curved pan.

6. When the cookies are done, set cookie sheet on heat-proof surface and **ask an adult** to help you slide hot cookies off pan with spatula or pancake turner and set them **immediately** onto curved surface of broom or curved pan, as shown. Leave cookies in this position until cold. Store cookies in airtight tin.
NOTE: If cookies cool too much to lift from baking sheet, they can be set back in the oven to warm for about 1 to 2 minutes.

BABAS AU RHUM

These light spongy *babas* or cakes are made with a yeast dough shaped to fit into a muffin pan. After they are baked, the cakes are soaked with a spicy orange-rum syrup. Children can use the fruit or rum extract listed in the recipe. Adults may prefer to substitute ½ to ¾ cup dark rum (about 185 ml) in the syrup (See note 8, page 11). Babas are easy to make. They take time, however, because the dough must rise twice, for a total of nearly two hours, so plan your time accordingly. They are worth the time, however, as they are a very impressive and delicious holiday dessert.

EQUIPMENT:

Measuring cups and spoons
2 large and 1 small mixing bowls
2 saucepans
Wooden spoon
Grater
Electric mixer with its own bowl
2 mixing spoons
Rubber scraper
Wax paper
Muffin tins—either 3″ diameter (7.5 cm) or 2″ diameter (5 cm)
Cake tester or toothpick
Table knife or fork
Large flat plate or pan, with at least a 1″ (2.5 cm) deep edge
Strainer
Plastic wrap

FOODS YOU WILL NEED:
Dough:
¼ cup granulated sugar (60 ml; 55 g)
¼ cup lukewarm water (60 ml)
1 package dry granulated yeast (¼ oz; 7 g) or equivalent amount of compressed yeast
¼ cup milk (60 ml)
4 tablespoons butter or margarine (60 g)
1 egg plus 2 yolks
1 whole orange
⅛ teaspoon salt (.5 ml)
1¾ cups all-purpose flour (435 ml; 285 g)

Syrup:
1½ cups water (375 ml)
1½ cups granulated sugar (375 ml; 315 g)
2 thick slices lemon
1 stick cinnamon
2 to 3 whole cloves
1 teaspoon orange, lemon, or rum extract (5 ml)

Ingredients:

(To make 9 babas 3″ [7.5 cm] in diameter or 20 babas 2″ [5 cm] in diameter)
Dough:
¼ cup granulated sugar (60 ml; 55 g)
¼ cup lukewarm water (60 ml)
1 package dry granulated yeast (¼ oz; 7 g) or equivalent amount of compressed yeast

How To:

1. Measure sugar and set it aside. Read *About Yeast*, step 6, page 11. Measure *lukewarm* (not hot!) water into small bowl. Sprinkle yeast over water and add 1 teaspoon (5 ml) from measured sugar.

   Set yeast aside for about five minutes, until it looks bubbly.

¼ cup milk (60 ml)
4 tablespoons butter or
   margarine (60 g)
1 whole orange

1 egg plus 2 yolks
⅛ teaspoon salt (.5 ml)
1¾ cups all-purpose flour
   (435 ml; 285 g)

4. Grease large clean bowl with a little butter or margarine. With rubber scraper, push all dough from mixing bowl into greased bowl. Cover with greased piece of wax paper and set bowl in a warm place to rise for about 1½ hours, or until it is nearly double in bulk. Then stir down dough (it will be too sticky to punch down with your hands) to remove excess gas bubbles.

2. Measure milk into saucepan and set it over medium heat until little bubbles form at the edges. Remove pan from heat and add butter. Stir until butter melts. Set pan aside to cool. Grate orange rind onto wax paper; save grated rind. Then cut orange crosswise into thick slices and save for use in syrup. Remove orange pits.

3. In electric mixer, beat egg plus yolks until light colored. Gradually add remaining measured sugar and beat well. Add cooled milk mixture, orange rind, and salt. Beat again. Test temperature of mixture with your finger. If it is lukewarm, or cooler, add yeast mixture and beat. Gradually add flour to mixture, sifting it into bowl. Beat slowly until flour is combined. Then beat about 4 minutes longer.

5. Preheat oven to 400°F (205°C). Grease muffin cups with butter or margarine. Spoon batter into cups, filling about ⅔ full. Cover with sheet of greased wax paper and set trays in warm place for about 30 minutes, or until batter rises *almost* to the rim of the cups.

Syrup:

1½ **cups water (375 ml)**

1½ **cups granulated sugar (375 ml; 315 g)**

2 **thick slices lemon**

2 to 3 **thick slices of orange saved from Step 2**

1 **stick cinnamon**

2 to 3 **whole cloves**

1 **teaspoon orange, lemon, or rum extract (5 ml)**

7. When baked, set muffin trays on a heat-proof surface to cool about 5 minutes. Use knife or fork to help you gently pry babas out of the tins. Set them *upside down* in a shallow flat dish or pan that has at least a 1″ deep edge. Babas are set upside down because their bottoms are more porous than their tops. Spoon the warm syrup over the babas continuously, until they are well soaked. Scoop up excess syrup from bottom of the dish. When you are sure babas are well soaked with syrup, turn them right side up in the syrup plate

6. Add a few spoons of water to any *empty* cups of muffin tray so they won't burn in the oven. Bake babas at 400°F (205°C) for 10 to 15 minutes, or until golden and a cake tester inserted in the center of a baba comes out clean. Prepare syrup while babas bake.

Syrup: Mix together all ingredients except extract in a saucepan and simmer over medium heat for about 10 minutes. Set a strainer over a bowl placed in the sink. Drain syrup through this strainer, using the back of a spoon to press liquid out of fruit slices. Discard contents of strainer. Stir extract into syrup, and reserve until serving time.

or pan. Pour over any remaining syrup. Cover them with plastic wrap and refrigerate until serving time. Remove from refrigerator at least 30 minutes before serving. Serve topped with syrup, if any is left over.

THREE KINGS' CAKE *(GALETTE DES ROIS)*

The *galette* is a flat French cake. On Epiphany, it is always baked with a *fève*, or whole bean, hidden in the batter. Originally, a tiny porcelain figure of Jesus was used, and for this reason the bean is still called a *Jésus*. The finder of the bean is called the King or Queen, (*roi* or *reine*) of the Bean and is given a gold paper crown to wear for the party. The king or queen chooses a royal mate and the couple exchange little gifts.

Our favorite recipe for Galette des Rois comes from Brittany, a region of northwestern France. This easy-to-make cake tastes like Scottish shortbread. It is cookie-like in texture, buttery in flavor, and decorated with a golden egg glaze. For Epiphany, bake it in a fluted tart pan. For other times, you can shape the dough into small flat cookies.

NOTE: This recipe uses four egg yolks. The whites can be used to make meringue shells for the French Christmas Ball, page 34.

EQUIPMENT:
Measuring cups and spoons
Electric mixer
Container for egg whites
Small bowl
Table fork
10″ (25.5 cm) fluted metal tart pan with
    removable bottom
Pastry brush
Sharp paring knife
Cake tester or toothpick
Wire rack
Flat serving plate

FOODS YOU WILL NEED:
4 egg yolks
1 cup plus 3 tablespoons granulated sugar
    (295 ml; 255 g)
4 cups all-purpose flour (1L; 500 g)
1⅓ cups unsalted butter, softened but not
    melted (2 sticks plus 5⅓ tablespoons;
    300 g), plus extra for greasing pan
1 egg, plus 1 teaspoon water (5 ml) and 1
    teaspoon sugar (5 ml) for glaze
1 dry bean

Ingredients:

How To:

(To make one 10″ [25.5 cm] cake or two thinner layer cakes)
4 egg yolks
1 cup plus 3 tablespoons granulated sugar (295 ml; 255 g)

1. Preheat oven to 375°F (190°C). Grease baking pan and set it aside. In bowl of electric mixer, beat egg yolks and sugar together 3 to 4 minutes, until very creamy and light colored (almost white). Turn off the

1⅓ cups unsalted butter, softened but not melted (2 sticks plus 5⅓ tablespoons; 300 g)

4 cups all-purpose flour, sifted before measuring (1L; 500 g)

1 dry bean

Egg glaze:
1 whole egg
1 teaspoon water (5 ml)
1 teaspoon sugar (5 ml)

SCORED DESIGNS

mixer and lift the beater. Now watch the batter fall back into the bowl. Mixture is beaten enough if it falls like a flat ribbon folding over onto itself as it lands.

2. Add butter and flour alternately, a little at a time, and beat slowly. Add in bean. Batter will be thick, almost like cookie dough.

3. In small bowl, use fork to beat egg with water and sugar to make the glaze. Press the batter into the buttered pan, flattening the top with the palm of your hand. Batter should be about ¾" to 1" thick (2-2.5 cm). Brush egg glaze over top of cake.

4. Make a design in glaze topping: Score top of cake by *lightly* cutting through only the surface layer, making a design of straight lines in a cross-hatch, Christmas tree, or star. Bake at 375°F (190°C) for 35 to 40 minutes, or until cake top is golden brown and the tester poked in cake center comes out clean. If making cookies, bake 20 to 30 minutes, or until tester comes out clean and tops are golden. Cool baking pan on a wire rack. When cold, **ask an adult** to help you remove the pan bottom from the fluted ring. To do this, set it flat on a wide jar as shown, so the ring drops down. Slide cake off bottom of pan and onto serving dish. Cut in wedges. Hunt for the bean!

CHRISTMAS IN ITALY

Christmas in Italy is a religious holiday. The twenty-four hours between December 23 and 24 are a time of fasting, when most adults eat no food. On the evening of the 24th, Christmas Eve, a yule log called a *ceppo* is lighted in the fireplace (or a symbolic yule log is formed from candy or cake) and the family gathers to admire the *presepio*, a nativity scene made of miniature sculptured figurines. After a twilight candlelighting ceremony, a tiny statuette of the infant Jesus is set into the manger, completing the *presepio*, and everyone is wished a *Buon Natale* (Good Christmas).

The fast is then broken with a banquet that is meatless because of the fast day, but includes many holiday specialties. These vary depending on the area of the country. For example, one will find *Panettone** (a sweet dome-shaped bread filled with fruit and pine nuts) in Milan, *Panforte** (a fruit-nut candy) in Siena, *Cenci* (fried dough cookies) in Rome, and everywhere, cornbread with raisins, *torrone* (honey-almond nougat), and almond ice cream called *Tortoni*. After dinner and the exchanging of gifts, the family goes to midnight mass.

At the big family dinner on New Year's Day, a special *Torta di Ricotta** (Christmas Ricotta Cheese Pie) is traditionally served. The next eagerly awaited holiday (for children especially) is Epiphany, also known as Befana Day, on January 6. On this day, the Three Kings brought gifts to the infant Jesus in Bethlehem. Italian legend tells that the Befana, a kindly old lady who wears a kerchief and carries a broom, was busy sweeping out her house when the Kings stopped in on their way to find the newborn Christ child. They invited her to go with them, but she said she was too busy working and turned them down. The next day, however, she regretted her decision and decided to go. Looking for a gift to take, she found some toys that had belonged to her own baby. Carrying the toys, she set out, but never found either the Kings or the Christ child. So Befana searches still, on each Epiphany, visiting every Italian child to see if he or she is the one she is looking for. In memory of Jesus, she always leaves a token of her visit: a gift for the good, or a lump of charcoal for the naughty. At festive Befana Day fairs throughout Italy, children visit "real" Befanas to ask for gifts, just as American children visit department store Santas.

ITALIAN CHRISTMAS TREE NAPKIN HOLDER

When a spring-type clothespin is sandwiched between paper Christmas trees, it becomes a decorative napkin holder for your Christmas party table.

Materials: Green construction paper, scraps of colored foil or gold stars or sequins, glue, ruler, scissors, wooden spring-type clothespins.

1. Cut a sheet of construction paper 3½″ × 4½″ (9 × 11 cm). Fold paper in half to 3½″ × 2¼″ (9 × 5.5 cm). On the upper half, draw the tree shape, as shown.

2. Hold both sheets of paper together and cut out two trees. Decorate the top layer with glued-on stars, or write a guest's name down the length of the tree and use it as a place card-napkin holder.

3. Glue the back side of the decorated tree to the top of the clothespin. Glue the remaining tree to the bottom of the clothespin, as shown, sandwiching the pin between the trees. Fold a pretty party napkin and clamp it between the "jaws" of the clothespin and set it on the party table.

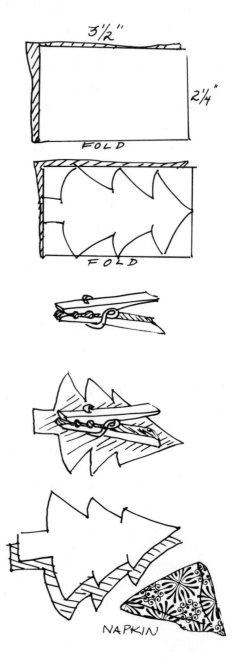

3½″

2¼″

FOLD

FOLD

NAPKIN

ITALIAN CHRISTMAS RICOTTA CHEESE PIE
(TORTA DI RICOTTA)

Ricotta, a type of Italian cottage cheese, is the main ingredient for this Christmas specialty. Depending on which region of Italy makes it, you will also find it contains chopped candied fruits and/or tiny chunks of bittersweet chocolate. Make it whichever way you prefer— our favorite is with the chocolate alone. Since the pie shell is pre-baked, it may be bought or prepared ahead and frozen until the day of serving, when you add the filling and bake it again.

EQUIPMENT:
9″ or 10″ pie plate (23-25.5 cm)
Large and medium-sized mixing bowls
Measuring cups and spoons
Fork or 2 table knives
Rolling pin
Wax paper
Aluminum foil
Pie weights (dry beans or rice)
Electric mixer
Pastry brush
Strainer

FOODS YOU WILL NEED:
Pastry:
1½ cups all-purpose flour (375 ml; 245 g)
½ teaspoon salt (2.5 ml)
2 tablespoons granulated sugar (30 ml)
7 tablespoons butter plus 2 tablespoons
    shortening (Crisco or lard) (135 g total)
1 egg yolk
3 to 4 tablespoons ice water (45-60 ml)

Filling:
3 eggs
1 cup granulated sugar (250 ml; 210 g)
1 cup candied mixed fruits, chopped (200 g) *or*
    ½ cup chopped semi-sweet *pure*
    chocolate (*mini-bits* or chopped block
    chocolate; 80 g). You can also use a
    combination of half fruit-half chocolate
1 pound ricotta cheese (2 cups; 560 g)
One 3-ounce package cream cheese, at room
    temperature (85 g)
1 teaspoon almond extract (5 ml)

Ingredients:

How To:

(To make one 9" or 10" pie [23 or 25.5 cm])
Pastry:
**1½ cups all-purpose flour
   (375 ml; 245 g)**
½ teaspoon salt (2.5 ml)
**2 tablespoons granulated sugar
   (30 ml)**
**7 tablespoons butter plus
   2 tablespoons shortening
   (Crisco or lard) (135 g total)**
1 egg yolk
**3 to 4 tablespoons ice water
   (45-60 ml) more if needed**

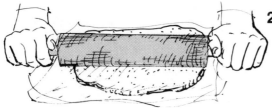

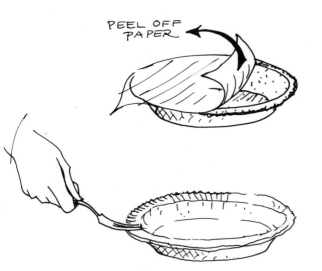

PEEL OFF
PAPER

1. First prepare pie shell. Note that it is partially baked before adding filling. In medium-sized mixing bowl, combine flour, salt, and sugar. Cut butter into small pieces and add, along with shortening. Mix together with fork or by cross-cutting with 2 knives, until dough forms rice-sized bits. Add egg yolk and only enough ice water to hold dough together into a ball. Do not overwork dough. Mix only until particles cling together. Preheat oven to 425°F (220°C).

2. Turn out dough onto floured piece of wax paper. Press into a ball. If you have time, wrap and chill in fridge for 30 minutes. Or, roll out directly between two sheets of floured wax paper. Roll until dough is a little larger around than pie plate when it is set upside down over dough (as shown).
   Peel off top paper, turn dough over onto pie plate, center dough, and peel off backing paper. Press dough into plate.

3. Fold up overhanging dough edges, making a neat rim. Flute rim by pressing it down at intervals with tines of a fork dipped in flour.

4. Cut a sheet of foil large enough to line the pie plate generously. Fold up foil edges and press

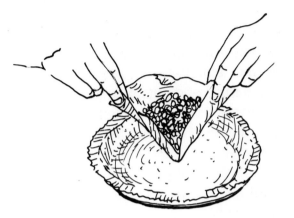

3 eggs
1 cup granulated sugar (250 ml; 210 g)

1 cup candied mixed fruits, chopped (200 g) *or* ½ cup chopped semi-sweet *pure* chocolate (mini-bits or chopped block chocolate; 80 g); you can also use a combination of half fruit-half chocolate
1 pound ricotta cheese (2 cups; 560 g)
One 3-ounce package cream cheese (85 g), at room temperature
1 teaspoon almond extract (5 ml)

bottom onto pastry-lined plate. Fill with 2 to 3 cups of weights (dry beans or rice used only for this purpose).

5. Bake pastry in 425°F (220°C) oven for 10 minutes. Remove pan from oven and set to cool. Carefully lift out foil filled with weights and pick out any stray bits that fell on pastry. When cold, pie shell can be wrapped in foil and frozen until needed. Be sure it is cold before adding cheese filling.

6. *Filling:* Preheat oven to 350°F (175°C). Beat eggs in large bowl of electric mixer. Then turn off mixer. Dip pastry brush into eggs and brush over bottom of pie shell to make it waterproof. Now add sugar to eggs and beat 2 to 3 minutes, until thick and light yellow.

7. Sprinkle about half the fruit and/or chocolate mixture over pie shell. Set remaining fruit or chocolate aside. Measure ricotta into a strainer and press out excess liquid over the sink.

8. To sugar-egg mixture, add drained ricotta, cream cheese, and almond extract. Beat until smooth. Stir in remaining fruit and/or chocolate.

9. Spoon mixture into pie shell and set in preheated 350°F (175°C) oven. Bake 40 to 45 minutes, or until puffy and golden. Serve warm or cold.

SIENESE NOUGAT CANDY
(PANFORTE DI SIENA)

Panforte di Siena is a famous Italian Christmas candy. In Italy it is rarely made at home because it is so widely available in stores packaged in thin, round boxes decorated with elaborate designs. This unique nougat is easily made of chopped fruits and nuts baked with honey and spices. It is so rich that it is served in very tiny cubes. Wrapped airtight, it will keep several months, and may be made well ahead of the holidays. *Panforte* also freezes well.

EQUIPMENT:
Measuring cups and spoons
Large saucepan
Sifter
Frying pan
Nut chopper
Wooden spoon
Grater
Mixing bowl
Lasagna-size baking pan (13½″ × 8¾″; 34 × 22 cm)
Toothpick or cake tester
Wire rack
Knife
Spatula
Foil or plastic wrap
Airtight container

FOODS YOU WILL NEED:
1 cup honey (250 ml)
1 cup granulated sugar (250 ml; 210 g)
1½ cups blanched almonds, toasted (200 g)
1½ cups hazelnuts, shelled, unblanched, toasted (200 g)
Grated rind of one large orange
1 cup all-purpose flour (250 ml; 165 g)
¼ cup Baker's unsweetened cocoa (60 g)
2 teaspoons cinnamon (10 ml)
½ teaspoon ground allspice (2.5 ml)
¼ teaspoon mace (1.2 ml)
1 pound candied mixed fruit, chopped (570 g)
Confectioners' sugar
Butter to grease pan

Ingredients:

How To:

(To make about 3 pounds [1.3 kg] candy)
1 cup honey (250 ml)
1 cup granulated sugar (250 ml; 210 g)

1. Butter a lasagna-size baking pan and set it aside. Preheat oven to 275°F (135°C). In large saucepan, combine honey and sugar and set on stove over low heat. Stir with wooden spoon for about 10 minutes, or until sugar melts. Remove pan from heat and set aside to cool.

1½ cups blanched almonds (200 g)
1½ cups hazelnuts, shelled, unblanched (200 g)
1 orange

1 cup all-purpose flour (250 ml; 165 g)
¼ cup Baker's cocoa (60 g)
2 teaspoons cinnamon (10 ml)
½ teaspoon ground allspice (2.5 ml)
¼ teaspoon mace (1.2 ml)
1 pound candied mixed fruit, chopped (570 g)

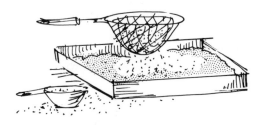

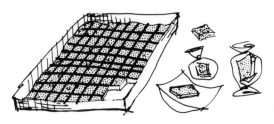

2. To toast nuts, measure almonds then hazelnuts (filberts) into frying pan, set over low to medium heat, and stir with wooden spoon until color *just* begins to change, about 3 to 4 minutes. Watch carefully, as nuts burn quickly once they get too hot. Place toasted nuts in chopper, and chop coarsely. Set aside in a bowl. Grate orange rind onto a piece of wax paper.

3. Measure flour, cocoa, cinnamon, allspice, and mace directly into honey-sugar mixture in pan. Immediately stir ingredients together well. Add fruit, then nuts and orange rind. Stir until well mixed, without big lumps of fruit.

4. Spoon mixture into buttered pan and spread evenly. Set in preheated 275°F (135°C) oven and bake for 45 to 50 minutes, or until a toothpick stuck in center comes out clean.

    Remove pan from oven and set on heat-proof surface. Sift confectioners' sugar evenly over top, just thick enough to cover candy. Now RETURN pan to oven and bake another 5 minutes. Remove pan from oven and set on wire rack to cool.

5. While the candy is still a little warm, cut with sharp paring knife into ¾″ (2 cm) squares. Wrap pieces in plastic wrap or foil and store airtight.

ITALIAN CHRISTMAS BREAD (PANETTONE)

Panettone is a fruit-filled, anise-flavored bread traditionally shaped into a round domelike loaf. You can also mold it into the form of a Christmas tree, decorate it with icing, and use it as a bright centerpiece for your Christmas dinner table. In Italy and in Italian communities around the world, *panettone* is sold at Christmas fairs and served at holiday tables. This dough rises twice, for a total of 2½ hours, so plan your time accordingly.

EQUIPMENT:
Measuring cups and spoons
2 small bowls
Small saucepan
2 large mixing bowls
2 cookie sheets
Wax paper
Scissors or sharp paring knife
Pastry brush
Whisk
Spatula
Wire rack

FOODS YOU WILL NEED:
Dough:
1¾ cups milk (435 ml)
5 tablespoons butter or margarine (75 g)
1 package dry granulated yeast
   (¼ oz.; 7 g) or equivalent amount of
   compressed yeast
¼ cup warm water (60 ml)
1 cup plus 1 tablespoon granulated sugar
   (265 ml; 225 g)
2 eggs plus 1 egg for glaze
4 to 5 cups all-purpose flour (500-750 ml;
   650-825 g)
1 teaspoon salt (5 ml)
½ cup seedless raisins (80 g)
½ cup candied mixed fruit (100 g) plus a
   little extra for decorating
½ cup shelled pine nuts (*pignolis*) (160 g)
½ cup blanched almonds, chopped (65 g)
½ teaspoon anise extract (2.5 ml) or
   2 teaspoons anise seed (10 ml)

Icing:
½ cup confectioners' sugar, sifted (125 ml;
   65 g)
2 teaspoons warm milk (10 ml)
¼ teaspoon vanilla extract (1.2 ml)

Ingredients:

(To make 2 round loaves or one big tree-loaf)

1¾ **cups milk (435 ml)**

5 **tablespoons butter or margarine, at room temperature and cut into small pieces (75 g)**

1 **package dry granulated yeast (¼ oz; 7 g) or equivalent amount of compressed yeast**

¼ **cup lukewarm water (60 ml)**

1 **tablespoon granulated sugar (15 ml)**

2 **eggs**

1 **cup granulated sugar (250 ml; 210 g)**

½ **teaspoon anise extract (2.5 ml) or 2 teaspoons anise seed (10 ml)**

1 **teaspoon salt (5 ml)**

4 **cups all-purpose flour (500 ml; 650 g)**

PUSH
TO
KNEAD

PUNCH!

How To:

1. In small saucepan, heat milk until tiny bubbles begin to show around the edges. Remove milk from heat, add butter or margarine, and set aside to cool.

2. Read *About Yeast*, note 6, page 11. In small bowl, measure yeast into *lukewarm* (not hot!) water. Add 1 tablespoon sugar, stir, and set aside until yeast looks bubbly—about 5 minutes.

3. In large mixing bowl, beat together eggs and 1 cup sugar. Add anise and cooled milk-butter mixture and stir. Test temperature of mixture with your finger. If it is lukewarm (not hot), add the yeast mixture and stir. Add salt and the flour, one cup at a time. Beat after each addition.

4. Add more flour, if necessary, to make dough form a ball. Sprinkle flour on work surface and your hands. Turn out dough ball and knead for about 5 minutes. To do this, read Basic Skills, page 15.

5. When dough is well kneaded and feels smooth, place it in a clean, oiled bowl, cover with oiled wax paper, and set in a warm place to rise until double in bulk, about 1½ hours. Lightly grease cookie sheets.

½ cup seedless raisins (80 g)
½ cup candied mixed fruit
  (100 g)
½ cup shelled pine nuts
  (*pignolis*) (160 g)
½ cup blanched almonds,
  chopped (65 g)

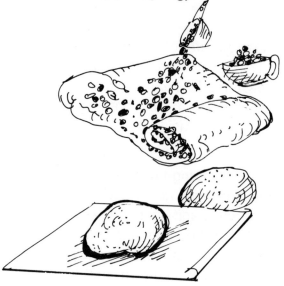

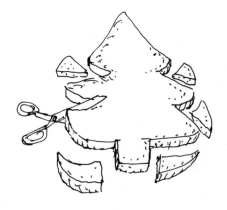

When time is up, PUNCH! down dough to remove excess gas bubbles. Turn dough out onto floured work surface. Press dough out into a broad flat rectangle and sprinkle on fruits and nuts. Roll dough up over them, then knead to distribute fruits and nuts evenly through dough.

6. You can shape *panettone* into round balls or make a Christmas tree. To shape balls, divide dough in half. Form each piece into a ball and set each one in the center of a greased cookie sheet.

   To make the tree, set all the dough on a floured work surface. Press dough into a basic triangular tree form. Use scissors to cut notches in sides for branches as shown. Cut a neat base on bottom edge. Gently lift tree onto the greased cookie sheet and rearrange shape.

7. Cover shaped dough with oiled wax paper and set in warm place to rise for about 1 hour, until *nearly* double in bulk. Preheat oven to 350°F (175°C).

Egg glaze:
1 egg plus 1 teaspoon water
(5 ml)

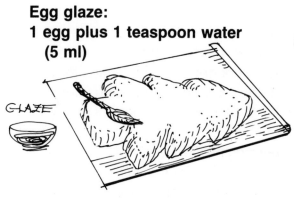

GLAZE

Icing:
½ cup confectioners' sugar,
sifted (125 ml; 65 g)
2 teaspoons warm milk (10 ml)
¼ teaspoon vanilla extract
(1.2 ml)

8. Make glaze by beating egg and water together in small bowl. Brush glaze over top of risen dough just before baking. Bake in preheated 350°F (175°C) oven for 35 to 40 minutes, or until golden brown and loaf sounds hollow when tapped with your knuckle.

9. Use spatula to slide *panettone* carefully off baking sheet to cool on wire rack set over wax paper. Make icing by beating all ingredients together in electric mixer. When *panettone* is cool, dribble icing over top. If you wish, decorative bits of candied fruit or halved, blanched almonds can be stuck into the icing before it hardens.

A VARIETY OF PANETTONE SHAPES:

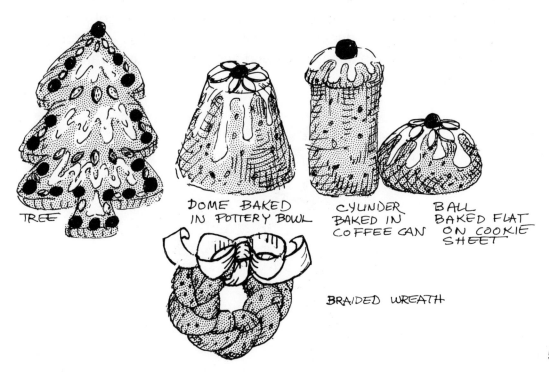

TREE

DOME BAKED IN POTTERY BOWL

CYLINDER BAKED IN COFFEE CAN

BALL BAKED FLAT ON COOKIE SHEET

BRAIDED WREATH

CHRISTMAS IN SCANDINAVIA

Long before Christ was born, people of the northern countries that are now Sweden, Denmark, and Norway held a celebration, called *yule*, at the winter solstice. This festival honored the sun, which they hoped would overcome the winter forces of darkness and night. Paying homage to the sun and light later became part of many Christmas customs.

In Sweden, the Christmas holiday begins on December 13 with *Luciadagen*, the Festival of Light in honor of Saint Lucia, the patroness of light. On this day in many Swedish homes, the eldest daughter dresses as Lucia, in a white gown with a crimson sash and wears an evergreen wreath containing real candles on her head. "Lucia" is followed by her younger sisters, also wearing white gowns, as they carry a breakfast tray of coffee and sun-colored, saffron-flavored "Lucia Buns" to their parents.

After weeks of preparation, the day of Christmas Eve finally arrives. It is the biggest celebration day, and begins when the family goes to church. When they return, they sit down to a Christmas banquet followed by gift giving around the Christmas tree. In Denmark, the traditional Christmas Eve feast includes either roast pork or roast goose stuffed with prunes and apples, served with red cabbage and Caramelized Potatoes.* In Norway, roasted short ribs may be added to the other specialties. In Sweden, the dinner takes the form of a *smörgåsbord,* or buffet, that includes a cured pig's head decorated with curlicues and scrolls of sugar icing, herring, salads, pork sausages, pâtés, spareribs, baked ham, red cabbage, and hot spiced wine, called *glögg*, to drink. This is followed by *lutfisk*, a lime-cured fish served with a creamed sauce and accompanied by a variety of home-baked breads.

SAINT LUCIA

The next course is the one most eagerly awaited by the children: the serving of Christmas Rice Porridge* (*Risengröd*), a treat found in all the Scandinavian countries. A whole almond is hidden inside this rich rice pudding and good luck goes to the one who finds it in his or her portion. The finder is entitled to a special gift, called the "almond gift." In Denmark, an extra portion of the *risengröd* is set out for the *Julenisse*, the good Christmas gnome who lives in the attic or barn and guards the family's welfare. If he is well cared for, the *Julenisse* brings the family gifts on this day. In Sweden, a bowl of rice pudding is set out for the *Jultomten*, the elf who brings gifts for all. The *Jultomten* looks rather like our Santa Claus, with his red suit, but he arrives in a sleigh drawn by Christmas goats instead of reindeer. Extra Christmas food is also given to farm animals, and sheaves of grain or blocks of suet and seed are set out on poles in the yard for the birds.

Buttery home-baked pastries and cakes are an important part of every Scandinavian Christmas. In Sweden, there is an old custom that the Christmas cake should be saved until spring, then thrown in front of the plow to insure an abundant harvest. Buttery Spritz Cookies* (*Spritsar*) shaped with a press are a favorite Christmas cookie. In Denmark, families bake extra-large batches of cookies—such as Danish *Sandkager**—for there is a saying that every visitor to the house must taste some homemade cookies. If they neglect to do so, "they will carry off the spirit of Christmas when they leave."

The Scandinavian Christmas banquet table is gaily decorated with candles, evergreens, bright red apples, bowls of nuts, straw stars, and figurines that include brightly trimmed gingerbread houses and straw Christmas goats tied with red ribbons. In Denmark, the table as well as the Christmas tree are decorated with red and white paper woven hearts filled with candies and nuts. After the feast, Danes wish each other *Glaedelig Jul* (Good Yule), while Swedes and Norwegians say *God Jul.*

JULENISSE

DANISH CHRISTMAS HEARTS

Red and white are the traditional colors for Danish Christmas decorations. Use red and white construction paper to make these woven paper hearts for tree ornaments. You can hang up one heart, or two stapled together to form a cone filled with candy and nuts.

Materials: Red and white construction paper, pencil, ruler, scissors, glue, darning needle, red carpet thread.

1. For each heart, cut out one red and one white shape as shown. Start with paper rectangles 3¾" × 6¼" (8 × 16 cm). Holding both red and white rectangles together, cut one set of short ends into a curve. Be sure both pieces are the same size.

2. Place the pieces flat and use a ruler to divide each straight short end into three spaces, each 1¼" wide (3 cm) as shown. About 3" (7.5 cm) in from the end, make a second set of marks with the same measurements, so they line up. Now connect the marks, drawing two straight lines, each precisely 3¾" (9.5 cm) long. On each piece, you should now have three strips, as shown, each 1¼" wide and 3¾" long (3 × 7.5 cm).

3. To weave, place the white piece over the red, lining up the straight edges as shown (a). Begin weaving the top white strip (marked x) and put it under the center red strip (b). Weave the second white strip under, over, under the red (c). The third white strip follows the first. Line up edges neatly and glue ends to hold.

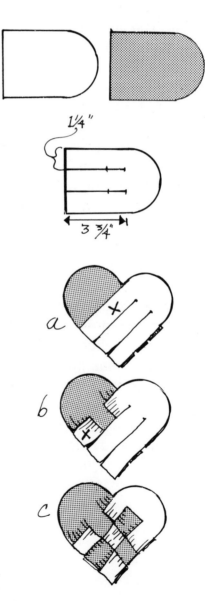

4. Thread a needle with carpet thread, stitch into the top of the heart, and pull thread up into a hanging loop. Remove needle and knot thread. To make a cone, staple together sides of two hearts.

CARAMELIZED POTATOES
(BRUNEDE KARTOFLER)

In this Scandinavian Christmas recipe, small boiled potatoes are coated with a butterscotchy caramel coating. They are delicious with roast poultry or meat and there is a bonus: leftover caramel sauce can be saved and later served over ice cream!

EQUIPMENT:
Large saucepan or Dutch oven
Colander
Long-handled fork
Table knife
Small saucepan
Measuring cups and spoons
Large skillet
Wooden spoon
Heat-proof serving bowl

FOODS YOU WILL NEED:
30 small unpeeled new potatoes (or larger
    boiling potatoes cut into small ovals)
½ cup granulated sugar (125 ml; 105 g)
½ cup butter (1 stick; 120 g)
Pinch of ground mace or nutmeg

Ingredients:

(To serve 10; allow about 3 potatoes per serving)
30 small unpeeled new potatoes, (or larger potatoes cut into small ovals)

How To:

1. Wash potatoes and set in large pot. Cover potatoes with water, bring to a boil over high heat, and cook about 20 to 25 minutes, or until soft when pierced with long-handled fork.

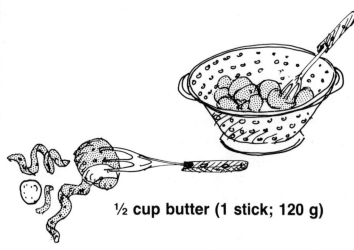

½ cup butter (1 stick; 120 g)

½ cup granulated sugar (125 ml; 105 g)
Pinch of ground mace or nutmeg

When potatoes are done, **ask an adult to** drain them in a colander. Peel when cool enough to handle.

2. Melt butter in small saucepan over low heat.

3. Measure sugar into skillet and set over low heat. Stir continuously with wooden spoon 3 to 5 minutes, until sugar melts and turns a light golden color. **Watch carefully:** if too hot, sugar will suddenly darken and burn. Slowly pour butter into melted sugar and stir. Add mace or nutmeg.

Add some potatoes and coat them with the sugar syrup. Spoon coated potatoes into a serving bowl. Keep warm in heated oven, and repeat to coat all potatoes.

DANISH SAND COOKIES *(SANDKAGER)*

In Denmark, Christmas *sandkager* are traditionally cut into wreath or heart shapes. For best flavor in these cookies, be sure to use unsalted butter.

EQUIPMENT:
Electric mixer or large mixing bowl and spoon
Measuring cups and spoons
2 teacups
Sifter
Wax paper
Rolling pin
Spatula
Cookie cutters
Pastry brush
Spatula
Wire rack

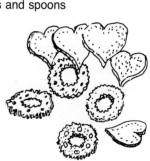

FOODS YOU WILL NEED:
½ cup unsalted butter, at room temperature (1 stick, 120 g)
1 cup plus 2 tablespoons granulated sugar (280 ml; 240 g)
1 egg plus 1 egg white
1¾ cups all-purpose flour (435 ml; 285 g)
¼ cup cornstarch (60 ml; 40 g)
2 teaspoons baking powder (10 ml)
Almonds, blanched, and halved or chopped, about one cup (250 ml)
½ teaspoon cinnamon (2.5 ml)

Ingredients:

(To make about 60 cookies)

½ **cup unsalted butter, at room temperature (1 stick; 120 g)**

1 **cup granulated sugar (250 ml; 210 g)**

1 **egg**

1¾ **cups all-purpose flour (435 ml;) 285 g)**

¼ **cup cornstarch (60 ml; 40 g)**

2 **teaspoons baking powder (10 ml)**

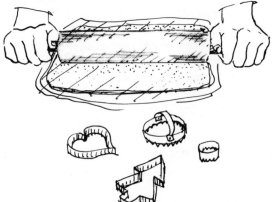

1 **egg white, lightly beaten**

1 **cup (250 ml) almonds, blanched and halved or chopped, for decoration**

2 **tablespoons granulated sugar (30 ml)**

½ **teaspoon cinnamon (2.5 ml)**

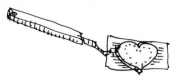

How To:

1. Grease cookie sheets and set aside. In large bowl *or* electric mixer, beat together butter and sugar until light and creamy. Add egg and beat. Sift in flour, cornstarch, and baking powder and beat very slowly until well mixed. Set dough in refrigerator to stiffen and chill for 30 minutes.

2. Break off about ⅓ of dough and roll it out between two sheets of floured wax paper until about ⅛" thick. Peel off top paper, cut cookies with cookie cutters, peel away excess dough. Dip spatula in flour, then use it to lift cookies onto greased baking sheet. Repeat with remaining dough. Preheat oven to 350°F (175°C).

3. With pastry brush, brush cookies with egg white, then decorate with whole or chopped nuts. In teacup, mix sugar with cinnamon. Sprinkle this over tops of cookies.

4. Bake cookies at 350°F (175°C) for 8 to 10 minutes, or until light gold around edges. Lift cookies with spatula and cool on wire rack. Store airtight.

SWEDISH CHRISTMAS RICE PORRIDGE
(RISENGRÖD)

This is the famous Christmas rice porridge served, with small variations, in all Scandinavian countries. An almond is hidden in the porridge and good luck goes to the finder. Swedes say whoever gets the almond will marry during the coming year. In some families, it is the custom for each person to compose a rhyme before eating this dish.

EQUIPMENT:
Measuring cups and spoons
Large saucepan
Wooden spoon
Serving bowl
Ladle
Soup bowls

FOODS YOU WILL NEED:
6 cups *cooked* long grain white rice, (1.5 L; 900 g) made from 2 cups raw rice (500 ml; 200 g)
2 tablespoons butter (30 ml) plus extra for serving
8 cups milk (2 L)
1 teaspoon salt (5 ml)
4 to 6 tablespoons granulated sugar (60-90 ml)
⅛ teaspoon cinnamon (.5 ml)
1 teaspoon vanilla extract (5 ml)
Nutmeg, freshly grated
1 whole shelled almond
Pitcher of milk or heavy cream (for serving)

Ingredients:

(6 to 8 servings)
6 cups *cooked* long-grain white rice (1.5 L; 900 g) made from 2 cups raw rice (500 ml; 200 g)
2 tablespoons butter (30 ml)
8 cups milk (2 L)
1 teaspoon salt (5 ml)
4 to 6 tablespoons granulated sugar (60-90 ml)
⅛ teaspoon cinnamon (.5 ml)
1 teaspoon vanilla extract (5 ml)

How To:

1. Cook rice according to directions on package. Set rice aside. In large saucepan, combine butter and milk and set over medium heat. Bring just to a boil, stirring with a wooden spoon. Turn heat to low as soon as milk boils. Carefully spoon in cooked rice, salt, sugar—more if you want it sweet—cinnamon, and vanilla.

Topping:
Granulated sugar, cinnamon,
** grated nutmeg, and butter**

1 whole shelled almond

2. Stir, then cook on medium-low heat, keeping uncovered mixture at a very gentle slow boil for about 45 minutes, or until porridge is creamy and rice is soft. If rice absorbs too much milk and mixture gets dry, add a little more milk. This is a creamy porridge, not a thick pudding.

3. To serve, pour hot porridge into serving bowl. Hide the whole almond in the mixture. Sprinkle top of porridge with a little granulated sugar and ground cinnamon as well as some freshly grated nutmeg. Top with several pats of butter. Ladle into individual soup bowls. Pour milk or cream over servings if you wish. Hunt for the almond!

ANNA OLSON'S SPRITZ COOKIES
(SPRITSAR)

In Sweden, these tender butter cookies make an important appearance at every Christmas gathering. *Spritsar* are formed with a cookie press, or *spritz-spruta*, that has a variety of disks to make hearts, stars, trees, or other shapes. If you don't have a press, the dough can be molded with your fingers.

EQUIPMENT:
Cookie sheets
Measuring cups and spoons
Large mixing bowl and large spoon
Sifter
Wax paper
Teacup
Electric mixer (optional)
Cookie press with disks (optional)
Pastry brush
Spatula
Wire rack

FOODS YOU WILL NEED:
1 cup lightly salted butter, at room temperature
    (2 sticks; 240 g)
½ cup granulated sugar (125 ml; 105 g)
1 egg, separated
1 teaspoon almond extract (5 ml)
2½ cups all-purpose flour (625 ml; 405 g)
Trimming (optional): raisins or halved blanched
    almonds, silver dragées, or tinted sugar
    sprinkles

Ingredients:

How To:

(To make about 60 cookies)

1 cup lightly salted butter, at room temperature (2 sticks; 240 g)
½ cup granulated sugar (125 ml; 105 g)
1 egg, separated
1 teaspoon almond extract (5 ml)
2¼ cups all-purpose flour, (560 ml; 365 g) plus extra if needed

1. Set out but do *not* grease cookie sheets. Set out cookie press if you have one.

2. Use mixing bowl and spoon or electric mixer to beat butter and sugar together until they are creamy. Separate egg. Add egg yolk to butter-sugar mixture, and save egg white in teacup for later use. Add almond extract and beat well.

    Sift 2¼ cups flour onto mixture in bowl and beat slowly until combined. Dough should be able to be formed into a ball with your hands. If it feels too sticky, add another ¼ cup flour.

3. Preheat oven to 350°F (175°C). If you are using a press, follow steps 4 and 5; if molding cookies with your hands, go directly to step 6.

4. If using press, read and follow manufacturer's directions. Select disk and fit it into end of cap. Turn disk until it locks (a). Replace cap. Unscrew plunger and plunger cap and remove them (b). Fill press slightly less than half full with dough. Press dough with back of spoon to remove air pockets. Replace plunger and screw down until it stops on dough. Stand press straight up on ungreased cookie sheet, resting it on its "feet." (c). Turn handle until dough comes out, forming cookie.

   Wait a few seconds for dough to adhere to sheet, then twist press slightly as you lift it straight up. You may also try turning plunger handle slightly as you lift. Cookie should stay flat. Practice makes this easy, though it feels awkward at first. Make a few test cookies.

5. Examine test cookies. If they did not press out easily, here are some things to try. Chill cookie sheet a few minutes in refrigerator. Turn plunger handle harder to force out more dough when forming cookie. If dough doesn't come out of press, it is too stiff and you should beat another egg yolk into dough. If dough is too sticky and soft, add more flour, a tablespoon at a time. In very hot weather, chill dough before pressing.

   As dough is used up, refill press about three-quarters full and continue pressing.

6. If you don't use a press, mold cookies with your hands. Add the full 2½ cups (405 g) flour to make dough slightly stiffer than for press. Flour your hands and roll bits of dough to form stars, wreaths, snowflakes, etc. Or roll out dough and cut shapes with cookie cutters.

7. Cookies may be baked plain or trimmed by brushing on lightly beaten egg white, then sprinkling with sugar, chopped nuts, raisins, halved almonds, or silver dragées. Bake cookies at 350°F (175°C) for 8 to 10 minutes, or until slightly golden around edges. Cool on wire rack and store airtight.

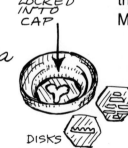

DISK LOCKED INTO CAP

a

DISKS

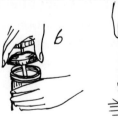

b

c

LUCIA BUNS

Saint Lucia is the patron saint of light. These yellow, saffron-flavored buns are served to Swedish families on December 13, Lucia Day, by a costumed "Lucia," the family's eldest daughter. They are shaped in spirals to symbolize the sun. Other traditional shapes are Lucia Cats and the Lucia Crown.

EQUIPMENT:

Small soup bowl
Measuring cups and spoons
Medium-sized saucepan
Slotted metal spoon or wooden spoon
Wire whisk
Large mixing bowl
Rubber scraper
Wax paper
2 cookie sheets
Tape measure or ruler
Pastry brush
Spatula
Wire rack

FOODS YOU WILL NEED:

1 package dry granulated yeast (¼ oz; 7 g)
    or equivalent amount of compressed yeast
¼ cup warm water (60 ml)
½ cup granulated sugar (125 ml; 105 g),
    plus 1 teaspoon (5 ml)
½ cup butter (1 stick; 120 g)
1 cup milk (250 ml)
Large pinch saffron *or* 4 drops yellow food
    coloring
½ teaspoon salt (2.5 ml)
1 egg
4 to 4½ cups all-purpose flour (1-1.5 L;
    650-730 g)
Vegetable oil for greasing pans and bowl
Seedless raisins, for trimming
1 egg, plus 1 teaspoon (5 ml) for glaze

Ingredients:

(To make about 12 buns)
¼ cup warm water (60 ml)
**1 package dry granulated yeast
    (¼ oz; 7 g) or equivalent
    amount of compressed yeast**
**1 teaspoon granulated sugar
    (5 ml)**

½ cup butter (1 stick; 120 g)
1 cup milk (250 ml)
**Large pinch saffron *or* 4 drops
    yellow food coloring**
½ teaspoon salt (2.5 ml)
**½ cup granulated sugar (125 ml;
    105 g)**

How To:

1. Read *About Yeast*, note 6, page 11. Measure warm (not hot!) water into small bowl. Sprinkle yeast over water, add sugar, and stir with spoon. Set aside for about 5 minutes, until yeast looks bubbly.

2. Add butter and milk to saucepan and set over *low* heat until butter melts. Do not boil. Remove pan from stove. Add saffron *or* food coloring, salt, sugar, and stir. Set aside to cool.

1 egg

**4 to 4½ cups all-purpose flour
(1-1.5 L; 650-730 g)**

PUSH TO KNEAD

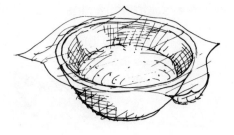

3. Break egg into large mixing bowl. Beat with whisk. Test temperature of butter and milk mixture. If comfortably warm to touch, pour mixture over beaten egg and whisk well. Test temperature again. If lukewarm (not still hot), add yeast mixture and stir all together.

4. One cup at a time, add about 2 cups flour to liquid in large bowl. Stir well after each addition of flour. Beat until dough is well blended and begins to look stretched. Add about 2 to 2½ more cups of flour, stirring until dough forms a ball.

5. Turn dough out onto well-floured work surface. Wash bowl for use in next step. Knead dough with floured hands for 5 to 10 minutes. To do this, read Basic Skills, page 15. Kneading is complete when dough feels and looks smooth and is not sticky to touch.

6. Grease large bowl with oil, then add dough ball. Turn ball over to coat with oil. Top with wax paper and set in warm place to rise until double in bulk, about 1 to 1½ hours. A good place for dough to rise is in the center of the oven, *with heat off*, with a pan of hot water set below dough on oven bottom.

65

7. Dough has risen enough when two fingers poked into the dough make holes that stay. Now, PUNCH! down dough with your fist, to knock some of the extra air bubbles out of the dough. Set dough on floured surface and knead two or three times. Grease cookie sheets and set them aside.

8. Shape dough into buns as follows and place shaped buns about 2″ apart on greased sheets. Buns must rise again before baking. Prepare egg glaze in teacup.

    Divide dough into 12 balls.

Egg glaze:
1 egg beaten with 1 teaspoon
water (5 ml)

9. Cover shaped buns with oiled wax paper. Set buns in warm place to rise about 1 hour, slightly *less* than double in bulk. Remove buns from oven if they are rising there. Preheat oven to 350°F (175°C).

10. Brush tops of all buns with egg glaze. Push down any raisins that have risen and popped off dough. Sprinkle granulated sugar over buns if you wish. Bake buns at 350°F (175°C) for 25 to 30 minutes, or until golden brown. Baked buns should sound hollow when tapped with your knuckle. Use spatula to remove buns to wire rack to cool.

GLAZE

ADD RAISINS

SUN SPIRALS:

Divide one ball in half. Roll each half into a rope 6″ to 8″ long (15 × 20 cm). Coil ends of rope as shown. Place strips back to back and pinch at center. Brush tops of each coil with egg glaze and press on raisin.

LUCIA CATS (Lussekatter):

Roll dough into 10″ to 12″ (25.5-30.5 cm) long rope. Curl or spiral each end in opposite direction as shown. Brush each curl with egg glaze and press raisins into centers.

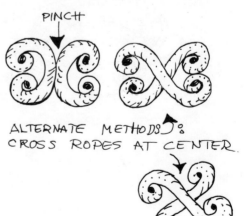
PINCH

ALTERNATE METHODS:
CROSS ROPES AT CENTER.

CHRISTMAS IN MIDDLE AND EASTERN EUROPE

Poland, Czechoslovakia, Hungary, Bulgaria, Rumania, Yugoslavia, and Greece are related to each other by geography and history. They also share many Christmas customs and foods. In addition, of course, each country has its own regional holiday traditions.

In Poland, for example, Christmas is an important religious holiday. The four weeks prior to Christmas are known as Advent, a fasting period during which no meat is eaten. Children eagerly await December 6, when Saint Nicholas visits them to bring holiday sweets and gifts which he leaves under their pillows as they sleep. Adults as well as children make decorations for the house and the Christmas tree, and by the time the holiday arrives, there are festive cut paper designs, straw stars and wreaths, apples, and toys everywhere. On Christmas Eve morning the tree is decorated and gifts for the family are set out. Also on this day, called *Wigilia*, Poles put hay under and around the dining table, as well as under the tablecloth, as a reminder of the stable where Christ was born.

When the first star appears in the sky on Christmas Eve, the Christmas Supper is served. Though meatless because of the fast, this is one of the year's most festive meals. The table is set with an extra chair for the Holy Child and an extra place for any stranger who may come by. Before serving dinner, the mother passes a special large thin wafer around the table. Each member of the family takes a bite from the wafer, then all kiss and wish each other a good year. The menu may include a beet borscht (soup) served with mushroom-filled dumplings, pickled beets, vegetables, mushrooms, egg noodles mixed with poppyseeds and raisins, cheese-filled pastries, fish such as carp, herring, or pike, sauerkraut, breads, fruitcakes, and a fruit compote. Dessert consists of cookies and small pastries called *Mazurkas*,* which are fruit- or nut-layered bars with various toppings. After dinner, families exchange gifts, then go to Christmas Eve Mass, called the Shepherd's Mass, or *Pasterka*. There is a folk-belief that only on Christmas Eve, at midnight, all animals can speak with a human voice.

Christmas Day is the time for visiting friends and relatives. At the Christmas dinner, a favorite specialty is hot almond soup called *Zupa Migdałowa*.* New Year's Eve is celebrated with a late dinner featuring a spicy meat and sauerkraut stew called *Bigos*, followed by champagne at midnight.

Czechoslovakia is one of Poland's neighbors. Here women and children make beautiful Christmas decorations, including delicate Meringue Snowflakes* and icicles to hang on the tree. *Kolaches,* a favorite Christmas pastry, are buns of sweet dough with a poppyseed or fruit filling.

In Hungary, Christmas Eve is a fast day that ends in a party at dusk. Families exchange gifts, sing carols around the decorated Christmas tree, and serve a festive meal. As in Poland, a sweet noodle dish made with poppyseeds or nuts is traditional, along with other specialties including fish cooked with paprika sauce and served with potatoes and fruit. The following day a much bigger Christmas Day dinner includes a roast chicken, turkey, or goose with gooseberry sauce, chestnuts, roast potatoes, stuffed cabbage, fruit salad, nut cake, and a Christmas Poppy Seed Cake (*Mákos Kalács*) made of sweet yeast dough with a poppyseed filling. The Hungarian New Year's menus are special because they are symbolic. On New Year's Eve one is served roasted game such as venison, duck, or wild birds in the hope that the creatures will "run off with the old year's troubles." The New Year's Day dinner highlights roast suckling pig because, besides being fat and prosperous, the pig personifies good luck.

Yugoslavia shares many Christmas customs with her neighbors to the north. Chief among these is the burning of the oak Yule log, a custom found in the British Isles, Germany, and Austria. In Serbia, a region of Yugoslavia, the Yule log is burned in the belief that one's prosperity in the coming year will be as great as the amount of light from the burning log. In cities where huge logs and fireplaces are impractical, oak twigs are burned on kitchen stoves as a symbolic gesture. As in neighboring countries, Slavs place hay around the house, the dining table, and under the Christmas tree during the holidays. On Christmas Day, the feast includes stuffed cabbage garnished with either sour cream or yogurt and garlic (depending on the region), roast pork, soup, vegetables, and pastries, including a cake that contains a hidden coin. The Serbian mother makes sure she is the cake cutter because she alone knows where the coin is hidden. She is careful to serve it only to the father or head of the family, for Serbian folklore warns that "money will go out of the house if a stranger is served the coin."

In Bulgaria, as in neighboring lands, hay is scattered around the house during the holidays. Bulgarians enjoy holiday feasting and, among other specialties, serve a Christmas yogurt cookie called *Masni Kurabii*.*

In Greece, Christmas customs vary from one region to the next, but Christmas Eve is universally the most important day of the season. Throughout the country, children go from house to house singing Christmas carols. Families fast all day, then go to midnight mass. After mass, they return for a special dinner. In Salonika, for example, this feast includes roast lamb and *Tzourakia*, a round sweet bread with a hard-boiled egg set in the top. The father blesses the family, then cuts and serves the bread. After dinner, family members share gifts and obey an old custom that requires a light, or fireplace fire, to be kept going all night to warm and welcome the Virgin Mary in case she should stop by, a symbolic reference to the journey to Bethlehem.

On Christmas Day, the holiday dinner includes *Christopsomo*, a sweet bread decorated with the Byzantine Cross, and *Kourabiedes*,* sugar-coated nut cookies studded with cloves to recall the spices brought to Jesus by the Wise Men. On New Year's Eve throughout Greece, people gather to eat, drink, and gamble—to test their luck for the new year. For this day they bake a special sweet bread called *Vassilopitta* (Saint Basil's Cake) in honor of Saint Basil, the patron saint of New Year's Day. *Vassilopitta* contains a hidden gold or silver coin, and the finder is promised good luck in the new year. Saint Basil's Day (New Year's Day) brings another favorite Greek tradition: the oldest man in the family distributes gifts to the children. Like Saint Nicholas of northern countries, Saint Basil was a bishop said to be a protector of the poor. He is believed to have given wedding dowries to poor young girls by secretly bringing them little cakes containing hidden coins.

CZECHOSLOVAKIAN MERINGUE DECORATIONS

In Czechoslovakia, women and children enjoy making elaborate Christmas decorations from a variety of materials. Like the Poles, they use straw as well as dyed corn husks to fashion the figures of the nativity scene.

Another of their specialties is a tradition passed down from one generation to the next: the making of delicate meringue snowflakes and icicles that are baked stiff and hung on the Christmas tree. These designs are surprisingly durable if handled with care.

EQUIPMENT:
Measuring cups and spoons
Electric mixer
Sifter
Plastic wrap
Wax paper
Aluminum foil
Cellophane tape
Ruler
Scissors
Pencil
Cookie sheets
Button Thread

FOODS YOU WILL NEED:
1 tablespoon egg white (about ½ white of one egg)
⅛ teaspoon cream of tartar (.5 ml)
1½ cups confectioners' sugar, sifted (375 ml; 190 g)

1. Make one or two paper cones to hold the meringue. For each cone, cut a piece of wax paper about 12″ long (30.5 cm). Fold this in half crosswise. Hold one finger at the midpoint of the folded edge (a), to mark the cone tip. Then fold up one short end, holding it as shown (b), while you wrap the other end tightly around, completing the cone. Keep tip pointed. Tape edge to hold together. Cut a *tiny* opening in the tip (c); opening size controls flow of meringue.

2. To prepare meringue, combine egg white and cream of tartar in bowl of electric mixer. Beat until white is fluffy. Slowly sift in sugar and beat until well combined. This quantity makes about ⅓ cup meringue, enough for about 30 icicles or snowflakes. Keep meringue covered with plastic wrap or it will quickly dry out.

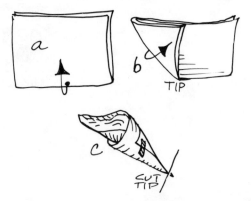

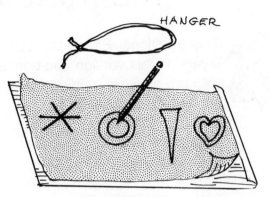

HANGER

3. To prepare several thread hangers for later use, cut 8"-(20-cm) lengths of thread, knot the loose ends together, and trim off excess beyond knot. You need one hanger for each meringue design.

4. Set a sheet of aluminum foil over each cookie sheet. With pencil, draw very simple guideline-shapes for your icicles, snowflakes, or wreaths, as shown. Leave space between designs for hanging threads to be spread out.

5. To make designs, spoon a couple of tablespoons of meringue inside a paper cone. Fold down open edges, roll over the fold to compress meringue and force it out the tip of the cone. Hold as shown, and draw over the guidelines drawn on the foil. With a little practice, this will be easy. You can make lacy icicles with figure eights close together, curly-edged wreaths, or solid, filled-in figures like snowmen.

   When each figure is completed, immediately set the knot of a thread hanger in the top and cover the knot with a small blob of meringue. Set thread hanger loop out flat above the design, as shown. Set tray of designs aside to dry in the air for at least six hours or overnight. If not completely dry, they will puff up when baked.

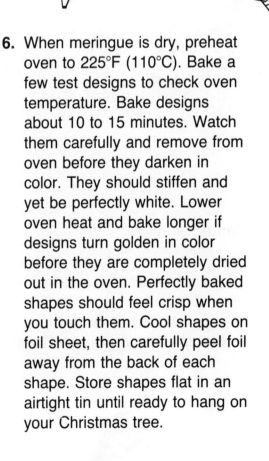

6. When meringue is dry, preheat oven to 225°F (110°C). Bake a few test designs to check oven temperature. Bake designs about 10 to 15 minutes. Watch them carefully and remove from oven before they darken in color. They should stiffen and yet be perfectly white. Lower oven heat and bake longer if designs turn golden in color before they are completely dried out in the oven. Perfectly baked shapes should feel crisp when you touch them. Cool shapes on foil sheet, then carefully peel foil away from the back of each shape. Store shapes flat in an airtight tin until ready to hang on your Christmas tree.

POLISH MAZURKAS *(MAZUREK)*

This traditional Polish bar cookie is often made with two or three layers. In this version, the bottom layer is a tender butter-nut cookie with two possible toppings: a simple coating of jam, or a rich, baked-on mixture of dried fruits.

EQUIPMENT:

Food processor, blender or nut chopper
Electric mixer
Large and medium mixing bowls
Measuring cups and spoons
Jelly roll pan 15½ × 10½ × 1″ (39.5 × 26.5 × 2.5 cm)
Rubber scraper
Spatula
Large spoon
Knife
Wire rack
Sifter

FOODS YOU WILL NEED:

Basic Dough:
2 cups shelled almonds, blanched and ground (270 g)
1 cup unsalted butter plus extra to grease pan (2 sticks; 240 g); or use half margarine
1 cup granulated sugar (250 ml; 210 g)
4 eggs
2 tablespoons milk (30 ml)
¼ teaspoon salt (1.2 ml)
2 cups all-purpose flour (500 ml; 325 g)

Jam Topping:
1 cup jam, such as apricot, raspberry, or strawberry (250 ml)
Confectioners' sugar

Fruit Topping:
½ cup shelled walnuts or almonds, ground (65 g)
1 cup pitted dried prunes, chopped (200 g)
1 cup dried apricots, dates, or figs, chopped (150 to 180 g)
½ cup seedless raisins (80 g)
½ cup candied lemon or orange peel, chopped finely (100 g)
2 eggs, beaten
6 tablespoons lemon or orange juice (90 ml)
2 tablespoons granulated sugar (30 ml)

Ingredients:

How to:

(To make about 70 bars 2″ × 1″ [5 × 2.5 cm])
2 cups shelled almonds, blanched and ground (270 g)

Basic Dough:
1. Preheat oven to 350°F (175°C). Grease jelly roll pan on bottom and sides. Grind almonds in food processor, blender, or chopper.

1 cup unsalted butter or use half margarine (2 sticks, 240 g), at room temperature
1 cup granulated sugar (250 ml; 210 g)
4 eggs
2 tablespoons milk (30 ml)
2 cups all-purpose flour (500 ml; 325 g)
¼ teapoon salt (1.2 ml)

FRUIT TOPPING

Jam Topping: Spread jam all over dough. Cool about 5 minutes, then cut in bars. Lift onto wire rack to cool further. When cold, sift on a light sprinkling of confectioners' sugar. You should be able to see some of the jam color beneath the sugar.

SIFT SUGAR OVER JAM TOPPING

2. In mixing bowl, beat together butter and sugar until light and smooth. One at a time, add eggs, then milk, and beat well. Add flour, a little at a time, beating slowly until combined. Stir in salt and ground nuts.

3. With back of large spoon, spread batter evenly over greased pan. Set pan in oven and bake at 350°F (175°C) for 20 minutes, or until top begins to look golden brown. Set pan on heat-proof surface and, while dough is still warm, spoon on the prepared topping of your choice.

Fruit Topping: See ingredients in *Foods You Will Need*. Chop all nuts, fruit, and peel as listed. Combine them in a bowl with eggs, juice, and sugar. Mix well. As soon as dough is baked, spread on an even layer of fruit-egg mixture. Return pan to oven to bake for an additional 20 minutes. Remove from oven, set on heat-proof surface, and cool 3 to 4 minutes. Then cut into bars about 1″ × 2″ (2.5 × 5 cm). To cut neatly, you can dip knife in water to dampen the blade. Lift out bars with spatula and cool them on wire rack.

BULGARIAN YOGURT COOKIES
(MASNI KURABII)

These delicate nut balls owe their tender texture to the yogurt, which is a dairy specialty of Bulgaria. Lard, also used in this recipe, is a rendered animal fat more commonly used than butter for baking in many eastern European countries.

EQUIPMENT:
Mixing bowl and spoon
Measuring cups and spoons
Food processor, blender, or nut chopper
Small saucepan
Cookie sheets
Spatula
Wire rack

FOODS YOU WILL NEED:
½ cup lard (125 ml; 150 g)
1 cup shelled walnuts, ground (125 g)
½ cup plain yogurt (125 ml)
½ cup granulated sugar (125 ml; 105 g)
½ teaspoon baking soda (2.5 ml)
1 egg yolk
1 teaspoon vanilla extract (5 ml)
½ teaspoon salt (2.5 ml)
2⅓ cups all-purpose flour, plus a little extra (580 ml; 380 g)
½ cup confectioners' sugar (125 ml; 65 g)

Ingredients:

(To make about 50 cookies)
½ cup lard (125 ml; 150 g)

1 cup shelled walnuts (125 g)

½ cup plain yogurt (125 ml)
½ cup granulated sugar (125 ml; 105 g)
½ teaspoon baking soda (2.5 ml)
1 egg yolk
1 teaspoon vanilla extract (5 ml)
½ teaspoon salt (2.5 ml)
2⅓ cups all-purpose flour, plus a little more if needed (580 ml; 380 g)

½ cup confectioners' sugar sifted into small bowl, plus extra if needed (125 ml; 65 g)

How To:

1. Preheat oven to 350°F (175°C). Measure lard into saucepan, set on stove over low heat until lard is melted. Set lard aside to cool.

2. Finely grind walnuts using food processor, blender, or nut chopper.

3. In mixing bowl, combine yogurt, sugar, baking soda, egg yolk, vanilla extract and salt. Beat, then add cooled lard and stir well. Stir in ground nuts and flour, adding one cup at a time. Beat after each addition. Dough should form a ball. If it is too sticky, add a little more flour, a tablespoon at a time, until dough can be handled easily.

4. To shape cookies, pinch off small lumps of dough and roll them in your floured hands, making small walnut-sized balls.

Set balls on ungreased cookie sheets and bake in 350°F (175°C) oven 15 to 20 minutes, or until lightly browned. Cool cookies on wire rack. When cookies are still slightly warm, roll them in the sugar. Store airtight, covered with more sifted sugar.

POLISH ALMOND SOUP
(ZUPA MIGDAŁOWA)

This soup is traditionally served hot for Christmas dinner. If it stands too long before being served, it tends to thicken almost into a pudding. If this happens, add a little more milk and reheat before serving.

EQUIPMENT:
Measuring cups and spoons
Large saucepan
Food processor or blender
Serving ladle
Soup bowls

FOODS YOU WILL NEED:
5 cups milk (1.25 L)
2 cups almonds, blanched (270 g)
1 teaspoon almond extract (5 ml)
2 cups *cooked* rice (500 ml; 300 g)
⅓ cup granulated sugar (80 ml; 75 g)
¼ cup seedless raisins (40 g)

Ingredients:

(To make about 8 servings; 2 quarts soup [1.90 L])
5 cups milk (1.25 L)

2 cups almonds, blanched (270 g)

1 teaspoon almond extract (5 ml)
2 cups *cooked* rice (500 ml; 300 g)
⅓ cup granulated sugar (80 ml; 75 g)
¼ cup seedless raisins (40 g)

How to:

1. In large saucepan, scald milk over medium heat. To do this, heat until tiny bubbles appear around edges of milk.

2. While milk heats, chop nuts very finely in food processor or blender.

3. When milk is ready, add all ingredients to saucepan, including nuts. Stir, then set on low heat and simmer soup about 5 minutes. Do not boil. Serve immediately, if possible. Or reheat with a little extra milk before serving.

75

GREEK NUT COOKIES *(KOURABIEDES)*

In Greece, these delicate sugar-coated nut balls are served at many festivals, but they have a special significance at Christmas, when each cookie is stuck with a whole clove, as a symbol of the spice brought to Jesus by the Three Wise Men.

EQUIPMENT:
Cookie sheets
Frying pan
Wooden spoon
Measuring cups and spoons
Electric mixer or mixing bowl and spoon
Food processor, blender, or nut chopper
Sifter
Wire rack
Wax paper

FOODS YOU WILL NEED:
1 cup almonds, blanched (135 g)
2 cups unsalted butter, at room temperature (4 sticks; 465 g); half margarine may be used
2 egg yolks
¾ cup confectioners' sugar, sifted plus extra for sifting over cookies (185 ml; 80 g)
1 teaspoon vanilla, almond, or brandy extract (5 ml)
½ teaspoon salt (2.5 ml), optional
1 teaspoon baking powder (5 ml)
4½ cups all-purpose flour (625 ml; 730 g)

Ingredients:

(To make about 50 cookies)
1 cup almonds, blanched, toasted (optional) and finely chopped (135 g)

How To:

1. Grease cookie sheets and set them aside. Preheat oven to 350°F (175°C). To toast, measure almonds into frying pan, set over medium heat, and stir with wooden spoon until nuts *just begin* to change color. Remove nuts from pan and chop finely in processor, blender, or nut chopper.

2 cups unsalted butter (4 sticks; 465 g); half margarine may be used

¾ cup confectioners' sugar, sifted (185 ml; 80 g)

2 egg yolks

1 teaspoon vanilla, almond, or brandy extract (5 ml)

½ teaspoon salt (2.5 ml), optional

1 teaspoon baking powder (5 ml)

4½ cups all-purpose flour (625 ml; 730g)

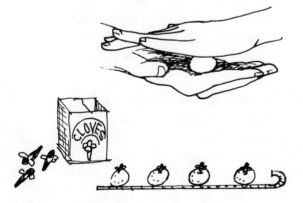

2. In electric mixer or bowl, beat butter until creamy. Sift in sugar slowly, beating after each addition. Add egg yolks, flavoring extract, and nuts. Beat well. Add salt, baking powder, and enough flour—little by little—to make dough workable. Turn off electric mixer and touch dough. It should not feel too sticky in your hands.

3. Flour your hands. Pinch off small lumps of dough. Roll balls the size of small walnuts. Place balls slightly apart on cookie sheets and stick a whole clove in top of each cookie. Bake in preheated 350°F (175°C) oven for about 12 to 14 minutes, or until lightly golden. Cool cookies on wire rack set over wax paper. Sift confectioners' sugar over warm cookies or roll them in a small bowl of sifted confectioners' sugar. Handle cookies carefully as they are fragile when warm. Store airtight with more sugar sifted on top.

CHRISTMAS IN GERMANY AND AUSTRIA

In European countries such as Germany and Austria, Christmas is such a big holiday that the baking often begins a month in advance. At the same time the baking begins, Advent wreaths appear, marking the official start of the four weeks before Christ's birth. Advent is especially important in Austria, where evergreen wreaths are displayed everywhere, gaily trimmed with four red candles, one to be lighted each Sunday until Christmas.

Children in both Germany and Austria look forward to receiving gifts and going to Christmas fairs on December 6, Saint Nicholas's Day. Saint Nicholas always appears at these fairs. He dresses in a bishop's long white robe, wears a tall red miter, or hat, and carries a sack of gifts. He rides on a horse or donkey, and travels with a black-robed companion whose job it is to spank naughty children with his birch switches. In some places, children set out their shoes filled with hay for the horse or donkey. Saint Nicholas comes in the night and replaces the hay with candies for the good, and, as a reminder to behave, a small bundle of birch twigs for the naughty.

Christmas Eve is the highlight of the holiday, when the parents finally show the excited children the secret they have kept hidden until this moment: the beautifully decorated Christmas tree. They sing carols around the tree, and enjoy opening the gifts supposedly left by the Christ child. After wishing each other *Fröliche Weihnachten* (Happy Christmas), they serve a special Christmas Eve supper featuring carp (a type of fish), and a variety of cookies and pastries that includes *Lebkuchen*, *Pfeffernüsse**, and *Butterhörnchen** (Viennese Nut Crescents). The holiday table might be decorated with an elaborately iced and candied gingerbread house. At midnight, the family attends a church service in honor of Christ's birth.

Christmas Day is the time for visiting and feasting. New Year's Day also has special customs. At the New Year's dinner, Germans serve a sweet, oversized "good luck pretzel" (*Neujahrspretzel*) that is made of sweet bread dough and is topped with icing and almonds. In Austria, marzipan appears in many dessert treats for the New Year: in candies such as Marzipan Stuffed Prunes*, and in the form of the pink marzipan "good luck pigs" with little gold coins in their mouths. The pigs are popular New Year's gifts, too. The pig is chosen as the symbol because it is as fat and prosperous as one hopes the New Year will be.

AUSTRIAN ADVENT WREATH

In Austria and in many other European countries, Catholics observe the coming, or "Advent," of Christ's birth by attending church every morning during the four weeks before Christmas. On each of the four Sundays, a special candle is lit on the *Advent kranz*, or Advent wreath. On the final Sunday, all four are lit.

Materials: 4 red candles and candleholders to fit them (or 4 red apples with part of core removed to hold candle), flexible wire, scissors, wire cutter, evergreen branches.

1. Wind wire several times around, making a circle about 12″ in diameter (30.5 cm). Set the candlesticks, without candles, evenly spaced around the wreath as shown. Fit the candlesticks between the wire loops, which you should pull apart slightly, making a hole, where the candlestick will fit. Remove candlesticks.

2. To attach greens, twist a short piece of wire over groups of evergreen stems, then twist them onto the wire wreath. Overlap greens, making a full, bushy wreath. Be sure to leave open the spaces in the wire where the candlesticks go. Bend any sharp exposed wire ends under. Be sure bottom of wreath is smooth enough to sit on table without marring surface.

3. Set candlesticks in wreath at marked spots, then add candles.

79

GERMAN SPICE COOKIES *(PFEFFERNÜSSE)*

These "peppernut" spice cookies with a sugar icing are easy to make and keep well. They are strong enough to be sent through the mail without crumbling.

EQUIPMENT:
Measuring cups and spoons
Large saucepan
Wooden spoon
Teacup
Rubber scraper
Grater
Large mixing bowl
Mixing spoon, table fork, teaspoon
Cookie sheets
Wire rack
Electric mixer with small bowl
Plastic wrap or foil

Frosting:
1 egg white
1 teaspoon honey (5 ml)
2 cups confectioners' sugar, sifted (500 ml; 200 g)
3 to 5 tablespoons pure lemon juice (45–75 ml)

FOODS YOU WILL NEED:
½ cup dark brown sugar (125 g)
¼ cup honey (60 ml)
¾ cup molasses, unsulphured (185 ml)
¼ cup butter or margarine (60g)
1 egg
3½ cups all-purpose flour (875 ml; 580 g)
1 teaspoon salt (5 ml)
1 teaspoon baking soda (5 ml)
1 teaspoon baking powder (5 ml)
1 teaspoon *each*: ground nutmeg, ground cinnamon, ground cardamom
¾ teaspoon ground allspice (4 ml)
½ teaspoon ground black pepper (2.5 ml)
¼ teaspoon ground cloves (1.2 ml)
1½ teaspoons grated lemon peel (7.5 ml)
¼ teaspoon anise seed, crushed (1.2 ml; optional)

Ingredients:

(To make about 85 cookies)
½ cup dark brown sugar, packed (125 g)
¼ cup honey (60 ml)
¾ cup molasses, unsulphured type (185 ml)
¼ cup butter or margarine (one half stick; 60 g)

3½ cups all-purpose flour (875 ml; 580 g)
1 teaspoon salt (5 ml)
1 teaspoon baking soda (5 ml)
1 teaspoon baking powder (5 ml)

How To:

1. Measure sugar, honey, molasses, and butter or margarine into large saucepan and set on stove over medium heat. Stir with wooden spoon until sugar melts. *Don't let mixture boil.* Remove from stove and set aside to cool.

2. In large bowl, combine flour, salt, baking soda, baking powder, spices, pepper, lemon peel, and—if you like—anise seed.

1 teaspoon (5 ml) *each*: ground nutmeg, ground cinnamon, ground cardamom

¾ teaspoon ground allspice (4 ml)

½ teaspoon ground black pepper (2.5 ml)

¼ teaspoon ground cloves (1.2 ml)

1½ teaspoons grated lemon peel (7.5 ml)

¼ teaspoon anise seed, crushed (1.2 ml; optional)

1 egg

Frosting:

1 egg white

1 teaspoon honey (5 ml)

2 cups confectioners' sugar, sifted (500 ml; 200 g)

3 to 5 tablespoons pure lemon juice (45–75 ml)

FROSTING

3. Use fork to beat egg in a teacup, then beat it into the cooled honey-sugar mixture.

4. A little at a time, stir flour-spice mixture into honey-sugar mixture that is in the large saucepan. Stir well. The dough will seem very soft. Chill dough 30 minutes in the refrigerator and it will stiffen and be easy to handle.

5. While dough chills, preheat oven to 350°F (175°C) and grease cookie sheets. Also prepare frosting by beating together all ingredients in electric mixer. Frosting should have a soft consistency, like a soft sour cream. Add more lemon juice if it is too stiff. Cover with plastic wrap until needed.

6. To form cookies, dampen your hands and roll lumps of dough into balls about the size of small walnuts. Set balls on greased cookie sheets and bake them at 350°F (175°C) for 12 to 15 minutes, or until light golden in color. Cool cookies on wire rack.

   Frost cookies while slightly warm. To do this, use your finger or a spoon to "paint" glaze-like frosting all over each cookie, *front and back.* Or coat several cookies at once by stirring them gently in a small bowl of frosting. Dry cookies on wire rack until frosting hardens. Store in airtight containers.

MARZIPAN-STUFFED PRUNES

This candy is easy for even the youngest member of the family to make. It keeps well, and in many northern European countries it is served at Christmas and New Year's celebrations.

EQUIPMENT:
Measuring cups and spoons
Paring knife
Frying pan
Small bowl
Wax paper
Airtight container

Ingredients:

(To make 36 stuffed prunes)
36 whole pitted prunes
36 whole almonds, blanched

8 ounces pure almond paste (220 g)
Green food coloring (optional)
1 cup granulated sugar, in small bowl (250 ml; 210 g)

FOODS YOU WILL NEED:
36 whole pitted prunes, dried
36 whole almonds, blanched and lightly toasted
½ pound pure almond paste, (220 g; sold by the 8-oz. can in specialty food shops)
Green vegetable food coloring (optional)
1 cup granulated sugar (250 ml; 210 g)

How To:

1. **Ask an adult** to help you enlarge the slit in the side of each prune by cutting it with a small sharp knife. Press a whole almond into the slit in each prune. Set prunes on wax paper.

2. Work almond paste (marzipan) with your fingers to soften it. Add a couple of drops of green coloring to tint the marzipan. Break off a small lump of marzipan and shape it into an oval. Press it into each prune on top of the almond. Roll stuffed prunes in sugar.

VIENNESE NUT CRESCENTS
(BUTTERHÖRNCHEN)

These tender nut cookies are rolled in powdered sugar while warm to give them a frosted coating. They are delicious made with hazelnuts (filberts), but you can also use walnuts or almonds to change the flavor.

EQUIPMENT:

Measuring cups and spoons
Food processor or nut chopper
Electric mixer or large bowl and mixing spoon
Cookie sheets
Small bowl
Sifter
Wire rack
Wax paper

Ingredients:

FOODS YOU WILL NEED:

1 cup shelled unblanched hazelnuts (or almonds or walnuts; 125 g)
1 cup unsalted butter (2 sticks; 240 g) at room temperature, plus extra to grease pans
⅓ cup granulated sugar (80 ml; 75 g)
2 egg yolks
1 teaspoon vanilla extract (5 ml)
2 cups all-purpose flour (500 ml; 325 g)
1 teaspoon baking powder (5 ml)
Pinch of salt
¾ cup confectioners' sugar, sifted (185 ml; 80 g)

How To:

(To make about 60 cookies)

1 cup shelled unblanched hazelnuts (or blanched almonds, or walnuts; 125 g)

1 cup unsalted butter (2 sticks, 240 g)

⅓ cup granulated sugar (80 ml; 75 g)

2 egg yolks

1 teaspoon vanilla extract (5 ml)

2 cups all-purpose flour (500 ml; 325 g)

1 teaspoon baking powder (5 ml)
Pinch of salt

¾ cup confectioners' sugar, sifted into bowl (185 ml; 80 g)

1. Finely chop nuts in food processor or nut chopper. Set aside. Preheat oven to 350°F (175°C). Grease cookie sheets.

2. In large bowl, beat together butter and sugar until creamy. Add yolks and vanilla and beat until fluffy. Stir in flour, baking powder, salt, and chopped nuts.

3. Pinch off small walnut-size lumps of dough and roll them on lightly floured work surface. Make rolls about as long and thick as your middle finger. Bend down ends of rolls to form crescent shape. Set rolls on greased cookie sheets. Bake at 350°F (175°C) for 10 to 12 minutes, or until pale golden. Cool cookies on wire rack.

4. When cookies are still slightly warm, *gently* roll them in sugar, then return to wire rack to cool. Store airtight, with extra confectioners' sugar sifted on top.

CHRISTMAS IN MEXICO

In Mexico, the Christmas holiday begins on December 16 with a procession known as the *posada* (literally meaning inn, or shelter). The *posada* is held in village streets, churches, and homes and commemorates the journey of Mary and Joseph from Nazareth to Bethlehem. The holy family traveled for eight days, and on the ninth, they found shelter in the stable where Christ was born. The procession is thus held for nine nights and consists of villagers carrying lighted candles and a *nacimiento*, or nativity scene, made of small statues. The *nacimiento* is often arranged on a wagon or cart pulled by children. The marchers, or pilgrims as they call themselves, go from house to house singing songs and asking for *posada*, or shelter. By prearrangement, they are turned down at many stops, until finally they are invited into one home and the real fiesta, or party, begins.

There is a fiesta on each of the nine nights, but the final one, on *Noche Buena* (Christmas Eve) is special. First there is a ceremony beside the *nacimiento* during which the little statue of Christ is set in the manger. Then there is the traditional party, where drinks, pastries, and cookies are served. These include the delicate, sugar-coated Mexican Nut Cookies* (*Pastelitos de Boda*). The favorite fiesta activity is breaking the *piñata*. Children are blindfolded, then take turns swinging a stick to try to break the decorative candy-filled *piñata* (pottery jar) which hangs from the ceiling. To make their task harder, the *piñata* is moved up and down by a pulley. The successful smash is followed by a mad scramble for the flying treats. While a *piñata* is broken on every *posada* night, the last, on Christmas Eve, is always the most exciting.

After church on Christmas Eve, a late-night Christmas feast is traditional. The house and table are decorated with brightly colored flowers and everyone is wished *Feliz Navidad* (Happy Christmas). Culinary specialties include Christmas Eve Fruit Salad* (*Ensalada de Noche Buena*), *Buñuelos* (fried dough buns covered with sweet syrup), and *Empanadas** (meat-filled turnovers). Some families exchange gifts on this night, while others prefer to wait until Epiphany.

On Christmas Day, the family feast includes a roast turkey covered with a spicy red pepper sauce served with tortillas. Young people enjoy drinking cinnamon-flavored sweet chocolate, the favorite beverage of the ancient Aztecs. Desserts always include *Buñuelos* and *Empanadas*, this time made with a sweet filling.

January 6 is the *Diá de los Reyes* (The Day of the Kings), or Epiphany. As this was the day the Three Kings brought their gifts to the Christ child in Bethlehem, this is the Mexicans' favored day for gift-giving. Young children set out their shoes so the Kings can fill them with gifts as they pass by. The favorite dessert on this day is *Rosca de Reyes* (Kings' Day Ring). It is a sweet fruit-filled bread made from a recipe similar to that for Italian *Panettone** (see Index), and formed into a ring shape. The ring contains a hidden whole dry bean that will bring good luck to the one who finds it in his or her portion. In addition, tradition declares that the bean-finder must hold a party for the assembled crowd on Candlemas Day, the festival of godparents on February 2. If a girl finds the bean, they say she will marry within the year.

MEXICAN FLOWERED NAPKIN RINGS

Gaily colored flowers are always a part of the Mexican Christmas celebration. Use bright red, orange, gold, purple, and green yarn to trim these easy-to-make napkin rings. The glue stiffens the cardboard and makes the rings durable enough to last for years.

Materials: Empty cardboard paper towel tube, scissors, ruler, pencil, brightly colored yarn scraps, white glue that dries clear (such as Sobo or Elmer's), toothpicks.

1. Cut the cardboard tube into rings about 2″ wide (5 cm). Make one ring for each napkin holder.

2. Draw a simple flower design in the central area around the ring. Allow room for a yarn border around both cut edges.

3. Draw lines of glue over the penciled lines, working on only one area at a time. Press cut lengths of yarn into the glued lines. Use the toothpick for a pusher. After the central design is outlined in glued-on yarn, fill in all background areas with glued-on yarn lines so that no cardboard is visible. Finally, glue a yarn border around each edge. Set rings aside overnight. Do not use until glue is completely dry.

NOTE: If you like, a strip of fabric or colored paper can be glued *inside* the cardboard ring to improve its appearance. To use, roll a pretty napkin and pull through tube as shown.

CHRISTMAS EVE SALAD
(ENSALADA DE NOCHE BUENA)

This traditional salad can be made with whatever variety of fruits you happen to have. You can use fresh fruits, or substitute canned fruits, drained of syrup.

EQUIPMENT:
Chopping board
Paring knife
Salad bowl
Measuring cups and spoons
Pitcher or jar for salad dressing

*The jicama, traditionally used in this salad, is a fruit that looks somewhat like a round potato. Its flesh is white, crisp, and sweet like a cross between an apple and a potato. Jicamas are available in most oriental markets.

FOODS YOU WILL NEED:
3 whole oranges, peeled, seeded, and cut up
4 slices fresh pineapple, cut up (or equal amount of canned pineapple cubes, drained)
3 bananas, peeled and sliced
One handful of seedless raisins
1 grapefruit, peeled, seeded, and cut up
2 large beets, boiled, peeled, and cubed (or equal amount of canned beets, drained)
2 large apples, peeled, cored, and cubed, or ½ a *jicama**, peeled and cubed
Lettuce
Shelled roasted peanuts, about a handful
1 pomegranate, peeled, seeds separated

Dressing:
Any vinaigrette (oil and vinegar dressing), *or* a light sprinkling of dark brown sugar

Ingredients:

(To serve 8)
See above list of foods

How To:

1. In large bowl, prepare and combine all fruits listed above. Keep beets in separate bowl. Set everything in refrigerator to chill until needed.

2. To serve, line large salad bowl with clean lettuce leaves. Add fruits and beets. Top with peanuts and pomegranate seeds and serve with dressing or sprinkling of brown sugar.

EMPANADAS

Pastry turnovers filled with meat or sweets, *empanadas* are Spanish in origin and are served throughout Central and South America. They are a Christmas specialty in Mexico, where they can be made very large and served for lunch, or shaped into bite-sized treats for snacks or hors d'oeuvres. We prefer to bake our empanadas, though they can also be deep-fried. After baking, they can be packed into plastic bags and frozen, though they are never quite as good as when freshly made. If frozen, reheat before serving.

EQUIPMENT:

Measuring cups and spoons
Large mixing bowl
Rolling pin
Ruler
Paring knife or 4″ (10 cm) round cookie cutter
Tablespoon, table fork
Garlic press
Cutting board or food processor
Large skillet
Teacup
Pastry brush
Cookie sheets
Wire rack

FOODS YOU WILL NEED:

Pastry:
2 cups all-purpose flour (500 ml; 325 g)
½ teaspoon salt (2.5 ml)
1 teaspoon baking powder (5 ml)
8 tablespoons butter or shortening (1 stick; 120 g)
6 tablespoons ice water (90 ml)
1 egg for glaze

Sweet Filling:
Any jam, preserves, or chopped fresh fruit mixed with sugar, raisins, cinnamon, and chopped nuts

Savory Meat Filling:
3 tablespoons oil for frying (45 ml)
1 pound lean hamburger (460 g) or other leftover meat or chopped poultry
2 cloves garlic
2 tablespoons chopped onion (30 ml)
¼ cup fresh parsley, chopped (60 ml) or 1 tablespoon, dried (15 ml)
2 to 3 tablespoons seedless raisins (45 ml)
1 hard-boiled egg, minced (optional)
10 green or black olives, diced
¼ teaspoon cumin (1.2 ml)
Salt and pepper
2 tablespoons tomato purée or tomato sauce (30 ml)

Ingredients:

(To make about 24 small empanadas [4"; 10 cm])

2 cups all-purpose flour (500 ml; 325 g)

½ teaspoon salt (2.5 ml)

1 teaspoon baking powder (5 ml)

8 tablespoons butter or shortening (1 stick; 120 g)

6 tablespoons ice water (90 ml)

Sweet Filling:

jam, preserves, or chopped fresh fruit mixed with some sugar, raisins, cinnamon, and chopped nuts

Savory Meat Filling:

3 tablespoons oil (45 ml)

2 cloves garlic, pressed

2 tablespoons chopped onion (30 ml)

1 pound lean hamburger (460 g) or other leftover meat or chopped poultry

¼ cup fresh parsley, chopped (60 ml) or 1 tablespoon, dried (15 ml)

2 to 3 tablespoons seedless raisins (45 ml)

1 hard-boiled egg, minced (optional)

10 green or black olives, diced

¼ teaspoon cumin (1.2 ml)

2 tablespoons tomato purée or sauce (30 ml) plus water if needed

salt and pepper, to taste

How to:

1. *Prepare Pastry:* In large mixing bowl, combine flour, salt, and baking powder. Add cut-up butter or shortening. Mix together with fork or by cross-cutting with two knives until dough forms rice-sized bits. Add a little ice water, stir, then add more water as needed *just* until dough forms a ball. Turn dough out onto a piece of wax paper and press it into a ball. Refrigerate until filling is prepared.

2. *Prepare Filling:* If using jam or preserves, set them out. If using fresh fruit mixture, chop fruit, prepare, and set aside in bowl

   For savory meat filling, add a couple of tablespoons of oil to frying pan along with chopped onion and pressed garlic. Sauté on medium heat for 3 minutes, stirring with wooden spoon. Add leftover meat or crumbled ground beef and cook, stirring occasionally, until meat loses raw color, about 5 minutes. Add all other ingredients and stir. If mixture looks too dry, add 2 or 3 tablespoons water to make it juicy. Cook together 1 minute. Remove pan from heat and set aside to cool.

3. *To Form Empanadas*: Grease cookie sheets. Preheat oven to 400°F (205°C). Work with a small portion of dough at a time. Set a piece of dough on floured work surface. Flour rolling pin and roll dough about ⅛″ thick (.25 cm). Cut dough into rounds the size of a teacup, about 4″ in diameter (10 cm). Have ready nearby a cup of water, a pastry brush, a fork, and a cup with one egg beaten in it, for a glaze.

   Put a full teaspoon of filling in the center of each dough round. Dip your finger into the water, then moisten a line around the dough edge as shown. Fold half the dough over, covering the filling and making a half-moon shape. Dip the fork tines in flour, then press them around dough edges as shown, to seal.

   Set completed *empanada* on greased cookie sheet. Brush tops with beaten egg glaze.

4. Bake *empanadas* in preheated 400°F (205°C) oven 15 to 20 minutes, or until golden brown. Serve warm. To prepare ahead, cool on wire racks, then wrap airtight and freeze.

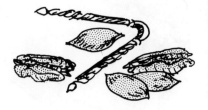

MEXICAN NUT COOKIES
(PASTELITOS DE BODA)

These cookies are traditionally served after the *posada* procession on Christmas Eve in Mexico. Their Spanish name literally means Brides' Cookies, as they are also served at weddings.

EQUIPMENT:
Cookie sheets
Large and small mixing bowls
Measuring cups and spoons
Large spoon
Sifter
Nut chopper
Electric mixer or slotted spoon
Wax paper
Spatula
Wire rack

FOODS YOU WILL NEED:
1 cup unsalted butter, plus extra to grease
    pans (2 sticks; 240 g), at room temperature
2½ cups all-purpose flour (625 ml; 405 g),
    sifted
½ teaspoon salt (2.5 ml)
½ cup confectioners' sugar, sifted, plus 2
    cups extra, sifted, for coating cookies (625
    ml; 250 g)
1 cup finely chopped nuts: pecans, walnuts,
    peanuts, or almonds (125 g)
1 teaspoon vanilla extract (5 ml)
¼ teaspoon almond extract (1.2 ml)

Ingredients:

(To make about 45 cookies)
1 cup unsalted butter, at room temperature (2 sticks, 240 g)
2½ cups all-purpose flour, sifted (625 ml; 405 g)
½ teaspoon salt (2.5 ml)
½ cup confectioners' sugar, sifted (125 ml; 50 g)

1 cup finely chopped nuts (125 g)
1 teaspoon vanilla extract (5 ml)
¼ teaspoon almond extract (1.2 ml)

2 cups confectioners' sugar, sifted into small bowl (500 ml; 200 g)

How To:

1. Preheat oven to 350°F (175°C). Grease cookie sheets and set them aside. In electric mixer or bowl with spoon, beat butter until creamy. Slowly mix in sifted flour, sugar, salt, nuts, and extract.

2. Flour your hands. Pinch off small lumps of dough, roll balls about the size of walnuts, and set them on greased cookie sheets. Bake in preheated 350°F (175°C) oven for 15 to 20 minutes, until faintly golden. Cool on wire racks. When still warm, gently roll cookies in sugar. Store airtight, covered with more sugar.

WRITE YOUR OWN FAMILY COOKBOOK

Every family has favorite recipes: your grandmother's apple pie, your aunt's walnut cookies, you mother's lasagna. What are *your* family's specialties? What are your family's holiday specialties? Where did these recipes, and the relatives who make them, originally come from? Concentrate on ethnic specialties, that is, foods unique to your own family, from whatever country or region they came from, whether Europe, Asia, or the American Ozarks. Getting to know a recipe can help you get to know the person who makes it as well!

Look into a recipe's history: where did that sesame cookie come from: "My aunt got it from her mother who made it when she was a child in Siena, Italy." And where exactly, is Siena, Italy? Look on a map. Ask other relatives. Look in an encyclopedia. You will quickly learn something about your family—where they came from, when, why—as well as the foods they like to eat. You can collect these recipes and histories into a family cookbook that you will treasure and want to make copies of to pass on to your own children.

To begin, make a list of your family's food specialties. Include your immediate family as well as aunts, uncles, grandparents, and cousins, too. Think of appetizers, hot and cold drinks, main course dishes (entrées), salads, soups, snacks, desserts, and candies. Think of holiday foods (Christmas, New Year's, Easter, and Thanksgiving), seasonal foods (summer berry favorites, winter "snow" candies, and fall pumpkin or nut treats), traditional cakes made for family birthday parties, comforting puddings made when you are sick and need pampering, brownies, cookies, turnovers you like to find in the cookie jar at grandma's house, homemade sweet breads or muffins you take in your lunchbox, taffy or candy you make with brothers or sisters on rainy days, fudge or other candies you make for holiday gifts. Think of favorite foods relatives make when you visit.

Start out as a reporter and ask a lot of questions. Get yourself a sharp pencil, a large sturdy envelope in which to keep any loose recipes people may give you, and a notebook in which to write the recipes and background notes. After you have gathered all your material, you can organize it into categories and then neatly copy it onto the pages of your book. Follow the format shown here to gather the information for each recipe.

Date:

Title of Recipe:

Name of Person Who Gave It to You:

Relationship to You:

Where and When This Person Was Born:

Recipe's History: What region or country did recipe come from? How did it come into your family? How has the recipe changed if it is no longer made in the original way? For example, "recipe first made with all meat, now we substitute vegetables because we are vegetarians." Is the recipe special for any holiday or family occasion?

Quantity Recipe Serves: For example "4 to 6 servings."

Special Notes: For example, "recipe can be frozen"; "this is a time-consuming recipe that takes 2 hours to prepare."

Equipment Needed: Special items like "rolling pin," "double boiler."

Ingredients: List foods and measurements as specifically as possible. Test your recipes if you can before adding them to the final cookbook.

How To: This is the procedure for making the recipe. Number the steps for ease in following recipe. Don't forget to include such details as: oven temperature; length of time for cooking; time required for rising dough, soaking dried fruit, defrosting frozen desserts; thickness of dough if rolling out pastry; safety tips—"stir candy syrup gently as splatters can burn."

How To Serve: Serve hot or cold; garnish or decorate with a special trim—"parsley, apple rings"; menu suggestions—what dish is usually served with—"Lasagna served with green salad and garlic bread."

To Organize Your Book: You can group your recipes by the type of dish (Drinks, Soups, Desserts, etc.), by the holiday (Christmas Foods), by the relative (Grandma Gold's Specialties), or by recipe's national or regional origin (Chinese, or West Coast Family Favorites). Sort out your recipes and notes.

Table of Contents: Make a Table of Contents, listing your categories and the recipes they contain.

Introduction: You may wish to write an introduction to your book that gives a brief background of your family and tells something about yourself, your age, where you live, and how you gathered the recipes for the book.

Illustrations: Plan to add illustrations and page decorations to your book. Show national flags, folk costumes, maps, even glued-in photographs or drawn portraits of relatives and special foods.

To Bind Your Book: After organizing the material, copy the recipes neatly onto the pages of a new notebook, or type or write them on separate sheets of paper. If not using a notebook, make front and back jackets by cutting two page-size pieces of cardboard. Cover both sides of front and back jackets with colored paper, glued-on wallpaper, or decorative, self-adhesive paper. Gather loose pages in correct order (Table of Contents, Introduction, Recipes) between jackets, and staple or sew along the left side as shown. If sewing, use strong wool or carpet thread with a darning needle.

For terrific gifts for other family members, duplicate the pages of your finished book on a copying machine, bind them together, and make extra books.

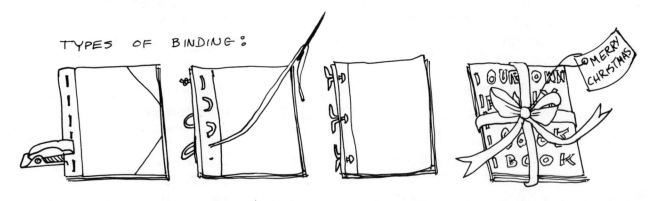

TYPES OF BINDING:

INDEX

Recipe pages are italicized.

Advent, 67, 78; Austrian wreath for, 79

Almond: French Almond Tile Cookies, 32, *36–37*; gift, in Scandinavia, 55; Polish Almond Soup (*Zupa Migdałowa*), 75; in Swedish Rice Pudding, 55, *61–66*; *see also* Nut Cookies

Ancient celebrations: Aztecs, 85; Celts, 8; Druids, 17; Romans, 8; Scandinavians, 8, 17

Babas au Rhum (French Rum Cake), 32, *38–39*

Befana Day, 43

Boxing Day, 19

Bread(s): Italian Christmas (*Panettone*), 43, *50–53*; Lucia Buns, 54, *64–66*

Brunede Kartofler (Caramelized Potatoes), *57–58*

Bubble and Squeak, 19

Butter, 10; measuring of, 13; substitutes for, 10

Butterhörnchen (Viennese Nut Crescents), 83

Cake(s): Fruitcakes, Individual English, *22–23*; Plum Pudding, Old English, *24–29*; Rum Cakes (*Babas au Rhum*), 32, *38–39*; Scandinavian customs about, 55; Three Kings' (*Galette des Rois*), 32, *41–42*

Candy: Marzipan-Stuffed Prunes, *82*; Sienese Nougat (*Panforte*), *48–49*

Cheese Pie, Italian Ricotta (*Torta di Ricotta*), *45–47*

Chestnuts: in French cooking, 32, 34; *Marrons Glacés*, 34; on ice cream sundae (*Coupe de Noël*), 32, 34

Chocolate drink, 85

Christmas Day and Eve customs and foods in: Austria, 78; Bulgaria, 69; Czechoslovakia, 68; Eastern Europe, 67–69; England

(and British Isles), 17; France, 32; Germany, 78; Greece, 69; Hungary, 68; Italy, 43; Mexico, 84–85; Middle Europe, 67–69; Poland, 67; Scandinavia, 54–55; Yugoslavia, 68

Cloves, 76

Cookie(s): Bulgarian Yogurt (*Masni Kurabii*), *74–75*; Danish Sand (*Sandkager*), 55, *58–59*; French Almond Tile (*Tuiles aux Amandes*), 32, *36–37*; German Spice (*Pfeffernüsse*), 78, *80–81*; Greek Nut (*Kourabiedes*), *76–77*; Mexican Nut (*Pastelitos de Boda*), *91*; Polish Bar, Mazurkas (*Mazurek*), 67, *72–73*; press, for shaping, 62–63; Scandinavian customs about, 55; Shortbread, Scotch, 30, *31–32*; Spritz (*Spritsar*), 55, *62–63*; Viennese Nut Crescents (*Butterhörnchen*), 78, *83*

Cones, paper, 70

Coupe de Noël (French Christmas Ball), 32, *34–35*

Craft projects: Austrian Advent Wreath, 79; Cookbook, writing your own, 92–94; Czechoslovakian Meringue Decorations, 70–71; Danish Christmas Hearts, 56; English Holly Place Cards, 20; French Epiphany Crown, 33; Italian Christmas Tree Napkin Holder, 44; Mexican Flowered Napkin Rings, 86

Crown, French Epiphany, 32, 33, 41

Decorations, Christmas: 8, 17, 20, 44, 56, 70, 79, 86; in British Isles, 17; in France, 32; in Germany and Austria, 78; in Italy, 43; in Mexico, 84–85; in Middle and Eastern Europe, 67–69; in Scandinavia, 54–55; *see also* Craft projects

Dough, yeast, 11, 15; rolling out of, 14

Egg(s), 11; separating of, 16

Egg Nog, 19, *21*

Empanadas, (Mexican Turnovers), 85, *88–90*

English Holly Place Cards, 20

Ensalada de Noche Buena (Christmas Eve Salad), 87

Epiphany (Three Kings' Day): cloves as symbol for, 76; in France, 32, 33; French Epiphany Crown, 33; in Italy, 43; in Mexico (Day of the Kings), 85; Three Kings' Cake, French, *41–42*

Flavoring, 11; alcohol used for, 11; artificial liquor extracts for, 11

Fruit: Cakes, Individual English, *22–23*; Christmas Cake, 18; *Ensalada de Noche Buena* (Mexican Fruit Salad), 87; Fruit Filling for Polish Bar Cookies, 72; Prunes, Marzipan-Stuffed, 82

Festivals. *See* Christmas; Holidays, ancient celebrations of

Flaming, of Plum Pudding, 18, 24, 29

Flour, 10; sifting of, 10, 13; types of, 10; weighing of, 14

French Rum Cake (*Babas au Rhum*), 32, *38–39*

Galette des Rois (Three Kings' Cake), 32, 33, *41–42*

Hard Sauce, 24, *29*

Health Food substitutions, 11

Hearts, Danish Christmas, 56

Hidden Coin (or token): in Greek Saint Basil's Cake (*Vassilopitta*), 69; in Mexican Kings' Day Ring (*Rosca de Reyes*), 85; in Serbian Christmas Cake, 68; in Swedish Rice Pudding (*Risengröd*), 55, *60–61*; *in Three Kings' Cake (Galette des Rois)*, 32, 33, *41–42*

Hogmanay, 19; Hogmanay Scotch Shortbread, 30–31
Holidays, ancient celebrations of, 8, 17
Holly, 8, 17, 20; English Holly Place Cards, 20
Honey, 10

Ice cream sundae (French Christmas Ball), 34
Icing: for Pfeffernüsse, 81; Hard Sauce, 29

Kourabiedes (Greek Nut Cookies), 76–77

Leveling measurements, 13
Light, Festival of (*Luciadagen*), 54
Lucia Day (*Luciadagen*), 54, 55, 64; Saint Lucia, 54, 64

Manger scenes, 32; *crèche*, 32; *nacimiento*, 84; *presepio*, 43
Marzipan, 78; Marzipan-Stuffed Prunes, 78, 82
Masni Kurabii (Bulgarian Yogurt Cookies), 74–75
Mazurkas, Polish Bar Cookies (*Mazurek*), 68, 72–73
Measurements, 12, 13
Meringue: Czechoslovakian decorations, 70–71; Nests (shells), 34–35
Metric measurements, 12
Mince pie, 18
Mistletoe, 8, 17

Napkin: Holders, Italian Christmas Tree, 44; Rings, Mexican Flowered, 86
New Years' Day and Eve customs and foods in: Austria, 78; British Isles, 18, 19, 30; France, 32; Germany, 78; Italy, 43; Poland, 67
Nougat, Sienese (*Panforte di Siena*), 48–49
Nut Cookies: Bulgarian Yogurt (*Masni Kurabii*), 74–75; French Almond Tile (*Tuiles aux Amandes*), 36–37; Greek

(*Kourabiedes*), 76–77; Mexican (*Pastelitos de Boda*), 91; Viennese Crescents (*Butterhörnchen*), 83

Onions, chopping of, 14
Oven temperatures, 11

Panettone (Italian Christmas Bread), 50–53
Panforte di Siena (Sienese Nougat Candy), 48–49
Pastelitos de Boda (Mexican Nut Cookies), 84, 91
Pfeffernüsse (German Spice Cookies), 80–81
Pies: mince, 18; Italian Ricotta Cheese (*Torta di Ricotta*), 43, 45–47
Piñata, 84
Plum Pudding: as Christmas pudding, 18; flaming of, 29; Old English, with Hard Sauce, 24–29; stirring of, 24
Porridge, Swedish Rice (*Risengröd*), 55, 60–61
Posada, 84
Potatoes, Caramelized (*Brunede Kartofler*), 55, 57–58
Press, for shaping cookies, 62–63
Prunes, Marzipan-Stuffed, 82
Pudding(s): flaming of Plum Pudding, 29; Plum, Old English, 24–29; Rice, Swedish Christmas (*Risengröd*), 60–61; stirring of, 24

Rice Porridge, Swedish (*Risengröd*), 55, 60–61
Risengröd (Swedish Rice Porridge), 55, 60–61
Rum Cake, French (*Babas au Rhum*), 32, 38–39

Salad, Mexican Christmas Eve (*Ensalada de Noche Buena*), 87
Sandkager (Danish Sand Cookies), 55, 58–59
Santa Claus: as Father Christmas in British Isles, 19; in Germany and Austria, 78; as *Le Père Noël*

in France, 32; as Saint Nicholas in Poland, 67
Sauce(s): Hard, 29; Orange-Rum, 38–40
Shortbread, 17, 21, 30–31; Hogmanay, 19, 30
Shortening, measuring, 13
Soups: Polish Almond (*Zupa Migdałowa*, 75; Porridge, Swedish Rice (*Risengröd*), 60–61
Spritsar (Spritz Cookies), 55; 62–63
Spritz Cookies, Anna Olson's (*Spritsar*), 55, 62–63; press for shaping, 62–63
Steaming: molds for, 28; of Plum Pudding, 28
Substitutions of ingredients, 10–11
Sugar, 10

Three Kings' Day. *See* Epiphany
Tile Cookies, French Almond (*Tuiles aux Amandes*), 36–37
Timing of recipes, 11
Torta di Ricotta (Italian Christmas Cheese Pie), 45–47
Tuiles aux Amandes (French Almond Tile Cookies), 36–37
Turnovers, Mexican (*Empanadas*), 88–90

Viennese Nut Crescents (*Butterhörnchen*), 78, 83

Wassail, 17
Wreath, Austrian Advent, 79; evergreens in, 8

Yeast, 11; Bread, Italian Christmas (*Panettone*), 50–53; Buns, Lucia, 64–66; Cake, French Rum (*Babas au Rhum*), 38–39; kneading dough with, 15; warm water used with, 11
Yogurt Cookies, Bulgarian (*Masni Kurabii*), 74–75
Yule (*jol, hjul*), 8; in Italy, 43; Norse yule logs, 17; in Yugoslavia, 68

Zupa Migdałowa (Polish Almond Soup), 75